Strategic Approaches

to

Starting, Growing & Optimising
BUSINESSES

Author: Mustapha Sani O

Strategic Approaches to Starting, Growing and Optimizing Businesses

International Standard Book Number 978-978-954-046-4

©Copyright 2016 by Mustapha Sani O

sasgob@yahoo.com

+2348175217867

Comments

This book is developed for:

- Students

- Staff at different levels

- Small start-ups

- Business owners

- Medium and Large companies

- NGOS & Government organisations

The key to developing a country is everyone's business. One way we can achieve this is by investing in the local economy (i.e. starting up or growing your own business). This will go a long way in contributing the economic growth and wellbeing of the nation.

-Mr Johnson Okeyniyi

Dedication

This book is dedicated to three groups of people. The first are individuals who have the great ideas and wish to start up their own businesses, but are having a hard time on how to go about it. The second group of people are those who already have their own businesses, but are passionate about growing their business. The third group of people are those who own large businesses or organizations or the ones who work in large Establishments or even government establishments (From top executives to managers, supervisors to the junior staff workers) and have a strong zeal to optimize performance in these establishments in order for the organization to provide more effective and efficient services, reduce waste, optimize performance for better customer/client satisfaction and improved profitability.

Acknowledgments

I give thanks to my God almighty that has kept me in good health and providing the wisdom, knowledge, understanding and direction and all my needs in completing this project.

Although this project required a lot of dedication and commitment, I wouldn't have been able to successfully complete it without the contribution of a number of special people.

My profound gratitude goes to my wife who was a great source of inspiration and very vital and much needed personal support to me who took her time to encourage me, took off some family responsibility to enable me complete this project.

I want to thank my Mum Mrs Felicia S O and my 3 beautiful kids, Ella, Mikkie and Joan whose encouragement have kept me going.

I wish to express my sincere gratitude to Mr Nosike and Mr Johnson Okeyniyi my academic advisors for their advice, support, guidance and encouragement.

Finally, I want to thank my friends and relations other contributors who have supported me in providing interview platforms in the development and eventual completion of this book.

Preface

Unemployment and poverty are major global challenges faced by many countries in the world. The associated problems include lower economic growth, increase in crime rate, increased use of drugs and alcohol, suicide, and other heath related issues. While the unemployed seek employment, the employee whose take home pay in most cases is not sufficient to take care of their basic needs seek ways to improve their income by various means like getting a better paying job, starting up a business, growing an existing one, or even optimizing the businesses in their various organizations as this will go a long way to increase their relevance, make them to be noticed. The associated benefits that accompany these activities include promotion in the office and an increase in their take home pay.

This book highlights innovative and strategic approaches used by professionals via a multidisciplinary approach to equip the reader in order to help them organise knowledge so that they can intelligently direct it through a number of problem solving techniques and the creation of practical plans of actions to the definite end of accumulation of funds.

This book explores available opportunities like the establishment or growing of one's own businesses, or even putting together initiatives in the very company or organisation you work enabling you to optimise your working environment and processes for better products, service delivery, customer satisfaction and profit the organisation.

Chapter One of this book introduces the reader to how some successful people have started with small ideas and grown them to become large conglomerates. It also shows the reader the relationship between increasing population and the increasing number of opportunities available with this growth in the context of the business environment for small scale or large organisations.

Chapter Two makes emphasis on the starting point which talks about how to conceive an idea meant to address real issues that will eventually grow into something big. It also gives you innovative strategies and methods on how to go about this endeavour.

Chapter Three talks about the importance of market research, how you can go about it and develop reports that will help you in the establishment of a viable venture.

Chapter Four focuses on strategic approach and methods to planning and development stages in business that can be applied in several areas be it a small, medium or large business organisation.

Chapter Five informs the reader about partnership in the business environment, why they are important and what qualities potential business owners should look for when selecting a partner for your business.

Chapter Six introduces you to funding, and various strategic approaches used by business owners to get funding for their venture.

Chapter Seven provides you with a strategic approaches a potential business owner can use to go about setting up the venture.

Chapter Eight emphasises business or organisation growth, its importance and strategic approaches to use when you want to grow a business

Chapter Nine makes reference to strategic approaches to business optimisation strategies that can be used by business owners or organisations. This system has been very successful in many manufacturing and production industries and if properly innovated can have limitless applications to help the user achieve success.

Acronym

AP	Action planning
BBD	Business backlog documents
BDP	Business Development Planning
BPMP	Business Project Management Plan
MCDA	Multi-Criteria Decision Analysis tool
MR	Market research
PDP	Personal development planning
POT	Project optimisation team
RCA	Root Cause Analysis
RE	Renewable Energy
SMART	Specific, Measurable, Achievable, Realistic and Time
SWOT	Strengths, Weaknesses, Opportunities and Treats

Table of contents

Chapter One: Introduction

Unemployment and poverty has been dreaded by many for a long time. In an effort to address these challenges, governments of many countries strive hard to educate a large number of their population, as they believe this can help eliminate these issues. The problems associated with unemployment and poverty include; lower economic growth, increase in crime rate, increased use of drugs and alcohol, suicide, and other heath related issues.

In an effort to eliminate unemployment and poverty, a lot of people seek ways to get alternative sources of income. These include getting involved in things like; contributing positively to their local community, starting up a business, growing an existing one or optimising performance in their respective places of work. In other to achieve this, they ask questions like:

- How can they contribute positively to their society?

- What kind of business they can start?

- How can they go about starting this business?

- How can they grow their businesses?

- How can they get funding and resources for their business?

- How can they work more effective and efficiently in their place of work to contribute to the growth of their organisation?

- How can they make better quality products or services?

- How can they provide better customer experience and satisfaction?

- How can they improve standards and profitability etc. and the list goes on and on and on.

Irrespective of which of the above options you choose, your most likely answer will be that you need to have a great idea. After this, you then need to invest time, money, coupled up with patience, research and planning for the success the endeavour. Furthermore, you need to ensure that you carry out the activities required to make this idea a success.

It is obvious that these things are important, but following history of how some small ideas grew into great businesses to become large conglomerates, you observe that having an idea was not all it took. You also need to believe that you have a workable solution to a problem that people will be willing to pay you in other to access that solution. This is a very important ingredient required to set up a successful venture. Like most philosophers will say you do not get paid for what you know, you only get paid for what you do or what you make others do, and you never know if you are capable of doing something successfully until you try doing it. Let's take a brief look at some examples down the history lane.

Fred Smith of Federal Express (FedEx)

The story of Fred Smith of the Federal Express serves as a good example of how the class work of a University undergraduate turned into a multibillion dollar enterprise.

Figure 1: Fred Smith

In 1965, an undergraduate Student of Yale University called Fred Smith was developing his economics course work on the topic: Exploring the process of transportation of goods in the United States, during his research he discovered that the shippers at that time were in the practice of making use of inefficient systems of transporting large parcels across the United States. After much investigation, he stumbled into a more efficient system.

He then nurtured, developed this idea over the years and after some years, he launched his company fully functional with his better efficient system via plane and called it the Federal Express. As at the early 21st century, the business was said to be operating in over 200 countries raking in an annual revenue of over $40 billion.

Ferrucio Lamborghini (Lamborghini)

Another example can be seen from a wealthy Italian farmer and part time mechanic who made tractors and owned a Ferrari. Back in his days, he used to have some problems with his Ferrari. These issues appeared to be similar to issues he had with his tractors (Clutch problems). Whenever he took the Ferrari for repairs, the service men would replace the problematic part, which after a while of usage, the car would develop a similar problem again.

Figure 2: Ferrucio Lamborghini (Lamborghini)

He decided to speak with the owner of the company (Enzo Ferrari), after a while of lobbying, he was able to gain audience with the owner of the company and he laid his complains to him. The discussion apparently didn't end the way he wanted it to. It was based on this development he decided to make a similar car that would address the clutch issues his on car (to his satisfaction), which he then called Lamborghini.

Colonel Sanders of Kentucky Fried Chicken (KFC)

Another example can be seen from the man who started the famous Kentucky Fried Chicken (KFC). A 65 year old man named Colonel Sanders had some financial difficulty, he then decided to try to put one of his passions into work. One of the things he did well was his chicken recipe which his friends liked and enjoyed so much.

Figure 3: Colonel Sanders of Kentucky Fried Chicken (KFC)

Due to his financial predicament, he decided to take a decision on his talent that would change his life forever. He decided to travel across the United States with the intention to sell his recipe to the owners of restaurants across the state. In return, he decided he would demand a small percentage of money from the sales.

He carried on with his plan but got series of rejections. After trying and failing over a thousand times, he finally got one acceptance from a restaurant. With belief, dedication and perseverance, he pursued his dream and today that idea has grown into the famous Kentucky Fried Chicken (KFC) with thousands of outlets in several countries around the world raking in billions of dollars annually.

These ventures and many more serve examples of how small ideas grew into great businesses to become large conglomerates.

Organising knowledge intelligently

According to Napoleon Hill in his book "think and grow rich" lot of higher institutions in the world over the years have been known to specialise in teaching knowledge but mostly are not inclined in the organisation or use of this knowledge to create wealth after school life. According to him, this issue has been a cause of much confusion for many graduates who believe that knowledge is power. They believe that as soon as they acquire the knowledge and graduate, their knowledge alone is supposed to enable them to start making money. But some soon find out that without getting a white collar job, things can get quite sketchy, making life challenging and also making it a little bit difficult to make money.

According to Napoleon Hill, knowledge was not defined as power in its entirety, rather, Knowledge is potential power. Knowledge will not attract money unless it is organised and intelligently directed through practical plans of actions to the definite end of accumulation of wealth (Napoleon Hill), which is where this is where this book comes in.

This book is structured in a way that the reader not only gains more knowledge, this book equips and enables the reader organise their knowledge so that they can intelligently direct it through problem solving techniques and the creation of practical plans of actions to the definite end of accumulation of money through various means like the establishment of their own businesses, growing an existing business or even putting together initiatives in which ever company or organisation you work, such that you perform effectively and efficiently to optimise your working environment and processes for better products, service delivery, customer satisfaction and profit for themselves or their organisation.

The Growing number of opportunities and Population growth

Over the years, research has shown that demographic variables like population growth has been seen as a possible determinant to demand and supply. While some research has shown that a declining population is usually associated to a reduction in demand for a lot of goods and services leading to the stagnation of many types of businesses, an increase in population is usually associated with an increase in demand and supply. This brings us to the optimism people have about increased opportunities associated with increase in population growth and increase in business opportunities (Coale 1960).

Population growth

The rapid increase in population and the rising number of unemployed youths in the world today is increasingly becoming a source of concern all around the Globe. In recent decades, population sizes in poor communities have often doubled and the unemployment rates relatively doubled resulting in economic growth issues in these countries (Bongaarts 2015).

Ever since the International Conference on Population and Development was held in Cairo in the mid 90's, (1994), reports from the Department of Economic and Social Affairs Population Division 2014, indicate that the world population has grown from 5.7 to 7.2 billion people, with a larger portion of the growth recorded in Asia and Africa (UN 2014).

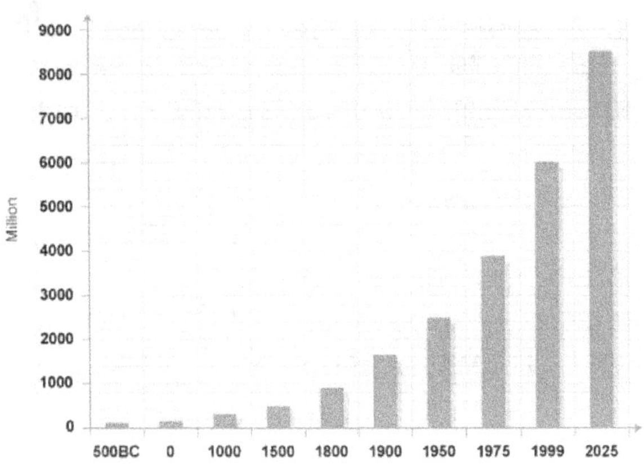

Figure 4: Population growth rate

According to UN (2014), while countries like Russia are experiencing an average annual percentage change of less than 1%, Northern America, Australia, parts of China and South America are experiencing an annual average percentage change of between 1-1.5%. On the other hand, India and others are experiencing 1.51 – 2% while Africa and the Middle East are experiencing an average annual percentage change of more than 3%. This shows rapid average annual percentage change in countries like Africa and the Middle East. The United Nations projected world population figures can be seen below.

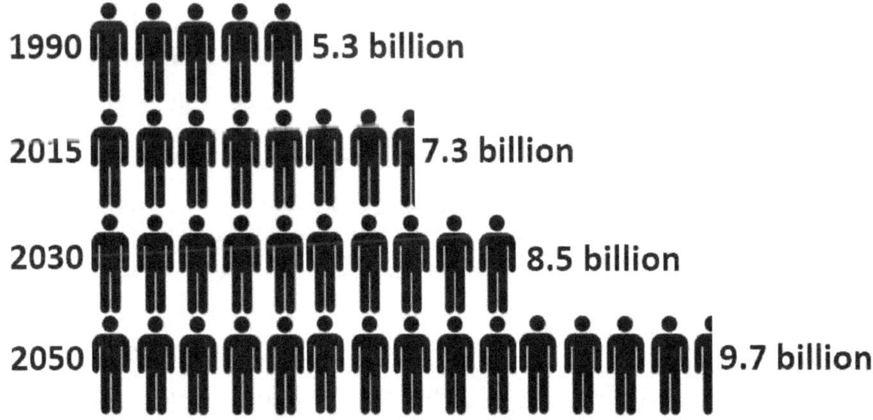

Figure 5: Projected world population figures (UN 2015)

As seen in Figure 5, the world population projections is expected to reach 8.5 billion by 2030, 9.7 billion by 2050 and 11.2 billion by 2100. From the analysis, it is expected that countries like Nigeria will overtake the United States to become the 3rd largest country in the world by about 35 years from now, while India is expected to surpass the population of China (UN 2015). Furthermore, the world population growth is expected to be concentrated in countries like India, Nigeria, Pakistan, Democratic Republic of the Congo, Ethiopia, Tanzania, the United States, Indonesia and Uganda.

Population growth and Urbanization

According to Buhaug, Halvard, and Henrik Urdal 2013, for the first time in many years, a larger proportion of the people living in the world today live in cities. This rapid urbanization will continue to grow at a rapid pace and is likely to reach about 3 billion between 2010 and 2050. The major reasons associated with this increase has been attributed to reclassification of rural land to urban land, high urban fertility rates and also rural to urban migration.

Studies have also shown that urban population have been known to enjoy a higher quality of life. In the developing world, there have been records of rapid development of slums to urbanised type settlements with large populations exceeding usually existing available resources, jobs, infrastructure, basic amenities and public services which often becomes a breeding ground for violence.

Regarding the wellbeing of most countries, the increase in population relatively increases the pressure on existing infrastructure like roads, schools, housing, industries and others bringing about the need to increase the rate of development of new infrastructures within those communities. This need has to be met as governments in these areas strive hard to develop these infrastructures. It is worthy to note that these challenges (if viewed from another angle) can be seen as opportunities for businesses to be established or existing ones upgraded to meet these needs.

Business and Market in context

Several researchers have defined business in different ways. However, the wildly used definition denotes Business as a financial activity. Thus an institution, organization or economic system where goods and services are exchanged for money can be called business. Below are definitions of business by various intellectuals:

Brown and petrello: "Business is an institution which produces goods and services demanded by people". It means business is an institution that produce goods and services needed by society. If the demand is increased, the producer also will increase production.

Griffin and Ebert (1996): "An organization that provides goods or services in order to earn profit". With this definition, business activity through the provision of goods and services aim to generate profit. An institution produce profit when "total revenues" in a period is higher than the "total cost" in the same period. Profit is the main feature of business activity, so that the profit can be expanded.

Musselman and Jackson:" An activity that meets the needs and desires of the community economic and organized a company to engage in such activities."

Stenford: "Business is all those activities involved in providing the goods and services needed or desired by people". It means business activities called that activities, which provide goods or services required and desired by persons of our society.

The online business dictionary defines a market as a place where forces of demand and supply operate, and where buyers and sellers interact (directly or through intermediaries) to trade goods, services, or contracts or instruments, for money or barter.

Markets include mechanisms or means for

1. Determining price of the traded item

2. Communicating the price information

3. Facilitating deals and transactions

4. Effecting distribution.

In a nut shell, the market for a particular item is made up of existing and potential customers who need it and have the ability and willingness to pay for it.

Types of Businesses

In the world today, there are different types of businesses an individual may decide to choose from, it may be owned by one single individual or several people with varying legal structures; it may be simple or complex in structure; it may also be large or small in size etc. Businesses also have different characteristics, advantages and disadvantages requiring require Small capital or large capital:

Some types of businesses include:

1. Sole proprietor

2. Partnership

3. Franchise

4. Limited liability

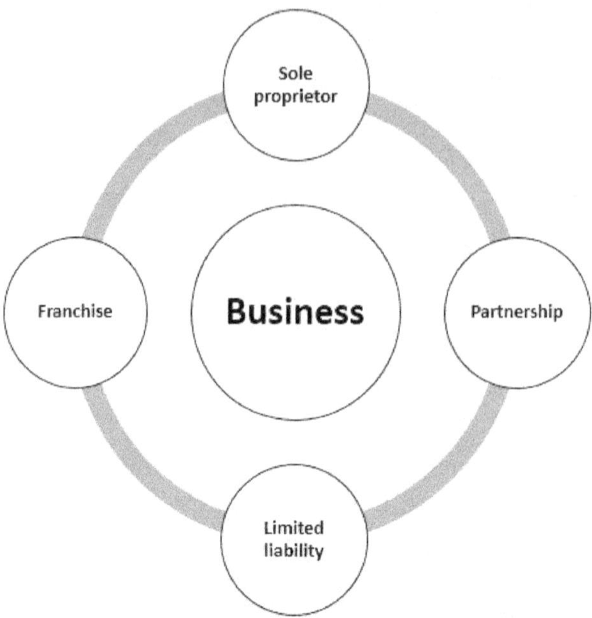

Figure 6: Types of businesses

Sole proprietor

This is considered the earliest and one of the most common types of businesses found around the globe today. It is owned and run by a single individual usually called the sole proprietor. Virtually all the decisions associated with the business are made by the owner who also bears all associated risks himself.

Advantages

1. This type of business is considered one of the simplest and easiest type of business to start up and dissolve

2. Here, the owner of the business practically controls all the operations and makes all the decisions

3. All the profits made from the business belongs to the owner of the business

4. This type of business is usually subject to fewer regulations in many countries

5. There is the tax advantage associated with this type of business

Disadvantages

1. There is the challenge of limited financial resources

2. When the owner is having some challenges that may make the owner unable to continue the business, there may be a problem of lack of continuity of the business

3. The owner is usually responsible for all obligations associated with the business

Partnership

The partnership business may be described as two or more persons coming together to establish a business with the sole aim of making profits. It may be commonly seen in professional services engineers, doctors, lawyers and accountants etc. Here, these partners share their expertise, skills and workload organising work schedules for the success of the business.

Partnership may also be in the form of:

1. Ordinary partnership

2. Limited partnership

Advantages

1. Funding is much easier to raise in this type of business compared to the sole proprietor. This is because there are

more than one person involved in the business there by increasing the sources of revenue

2. Here, financial institutions like banks and investment houses will be more willing to extend credit facilities to partnership businesses compared to the sole proprietor type of business

3. Due to specialisation, expertize and skills, the partnership type of business is usually more effective and efficient to operations compared to the sole proprietor type of business

4. Here, employees are usually more motivated to the this business type by the inventive to become partners

5. There is usually greater continuity in this type of business compared to the sole proprietor type of business

Disadvantages

1. Here, the partners are in most cases jointly responsible for all obligations associated with the business

2. There is usually the problem of delay in decision making and policy implementation as partners have to seek consent between each other before decisions are made

3. In most cases, partners have to agree in other to make decisions together. This, in some cases may bring about misunderstanding, disputes or conflicts between the partners and may eventually lead to the dissolving of the partnership business

Limited liability Company (LLC)

A Limited liability Company (LLC) can be described as a corporate structure in which the members of the company cannot be held liable for the company's debts or liabilities. However, studies have shown that these LLC's appear to differ slightly from one country to another.

Advantages

1. This type of business usually has access to a lot of financial resources. This is because, the business involves large numbers of people coming together to form the business and this usually results in the contribution of huge sums of money from members forming the business.

2. Due to organised management and specialization, financial institution like banks and investment houses in most cases are more inclined to extend credit facilities to them.

Disadvantages

1. In this type of business, regular reporting to governmental bodies is usually required.

2. Here, Interests are not freely transferable, rather, transfer of interests may be subject to securities law regulation.

3. In most cases, formalities are required for organization and operation.

Franchise

Franchises can be described as the system whereby an individual or group of individuals enter into a licencing agreement with other successful business models in other to buy the right to trade under a well-known brand name in a particular location.

Advantages

1. In this scenario, the new business enjoys the benefits attached to the already established business. Here, the goods, products or services enjoy wide spread brand name recognition.

2. Since the already established brand has proven goods, products or services, a franchise typically increases the chances of success of the new business due to an already established brand.

3. In most cases, a level of protection is spelt out in the franchise agreement. This protects the business, setting a standard for the franchise to offer high quality and high level of consistency.

Disadvantages

1. In some instances, franchises may perform poorly when there is a damaged wide range image that may result from unforeseen challenges e.g. Default in environmental standards, litigation against parent Franchise Company.

2. Franchise fee are often very high, as franchisees are required to pay for royalties, advertising and other fee in addition to the initial franchise fee.

Business failure

Definition: Business failure can be described as the closure of a business or the cessation of business activity. This may be as a result of the inability for the business to make enough profits to cover its operations and its expenses. It may also be as a result of the death of the owner without proper arrangements for continuation of the business. Business failure may arise from several reasons that may seem insignificant early in the business.

However, if these issues are not kept in check or addressed at the early stages of the business, it may result in poor performance of the business or eventually lead to a total and complete failure and ultimately the closure of the business.

Causes of business failure I (The broader perspective)

When setting up a business, focusing on the problems associated with the business is not what one should put all their attention to. However, knowing and being aware of these problems is important as they will aid you in the achieving success in the business. Research has shown that there are several reasons why a business may fail. It may be as a result of some uncontrollable circumstances or possibly from issues that may have easily being addressed earlier in the business. Some causes of business failure include:

- As a result of wars

- Recessions in the country

- Due to High taxation or high interest rates

- Excessive government regulations,

- Court order and other litigation issues

Causes of business failure II (based on survey results from this book)

During the development of book, we conducted a survey of some challenges businesses face within our locality. During this survey, we approached some individuals who had previously closed down their business in other to start another kind of business. The investigations revealed the following:

- No access to finance to support the business

- No access to some important equipment's they needed

- Due to poor management decisions

- Lack of capacity/skills development

- No electricity

- Lack of good transportation for the business

- No access to the market

- No access to suitable land or workspace

- Lack of business infrastructure

Causes of business failure III (Other researchers view)

We further researched into some of the problems businesses faced that may have resulted in business failure via previous studies carried out by various researchers and found out the following:

- Inability of the business owner to develop a good vision and Business Idea

- Inability of the business owner to raise Capital for your Start-up

- The Inability of the business to compete with other similar businesses

- Lack of experience on the business owner

- Lack of or insufficient capital

- Due to poor inventory management

- Due to unexpected growth

- Inability of the business owner to assemble a good Business Team

- Inability of the business owner to find a suitable location for the business

- Employing Employees with bad attitudes

- Inability of the business owner to resourcefully deal with Competition

- Inability of the business owner to deal with unforeseen Business Challenges and Expenses

- Inability of the business owner keep up with Industrial Changes and Trends

Ways to avert business failures

There are several ways one can avert failure in their business. More often than not, it is important to understand the business environment, the customers and observe how other successful business owners in the same field have succeeded in the past. In this book, we identify some of the key strategic approaches used by successful businesses and entrepreneurs over the years. Based on investigations, research studies and latest surveys, we found out the following:

- Successful businesses usually conduct critical and unbiased analysis before decisions are made. They are also carefully take into considerations long term and short term effects of the decisions before they are made.

- Successful businesses prepare for failure such that when it eventually shows up, they have a plan B to avert the failure and increase their chances of success in the endeavour

- Successful businesses carefully watch their cash flow such that there is little or no waste of resources.

- Successful businesses ensure that they are up to date and moving the business with the trend

- Successful businesses ensure that their marketing and sales budget are adequate

- Successful businesses develop innovative strategies to build very good relationship with their employees and customers

- Successful businesses ensure that there is proper planning for the future rather than predicting it.

- Successful businesses have it in mind that the market is a typical war zone, thus they ensure that they make adequate provision for marketing their business so that their product remains relevant in the market

- Successful businesses understand the realities in the industry and ensure that they work with that mind set

- Successful businesses ensure that they use the principles of successful businesses in reality, theory and research to stay successful

- Successful businesses ensure that there is proper planning of resources and borrowing what will be adequate for the business (not too much or too little)

- Successful businesses understand the difference between a business professional and a volunteer for example, when you are getting paid for your product or service, you are a professional. But when you are not getting paid for your product or services, you are a volunteer

- Successful entrepreneurs ensure that they keep their personal assets and business separate from one another

The role of small businesses in the growth of the economy of a nation

The role of small businesses in the growth of the economy of a Nation cannot be over emphasized. Over the years, traditional approaches to economic development used by Governments of many Nations was achieved by attracting large enterprises with financial incentives, tax breaks and other inducements. However, recent research shows that a growing number of economic development experts are deserting these traditional approaches, because, economic development strategies targeted at attracting large companies are usually successful but come at great costs. The results of years of studies by these experts reveal that in other to develop a more sustainable system, governments should redirect their interest to encouraging and building small scale business from ground up such that these systems will consequently support and supplement the growth of these large enterprises.

Some ways to achieve this is by providing incentives to support and encourage small start-ups and supporting the growth of small and medium businesses. These businesses are considered the backbone of the local economy and supporting them will go a long way in contributing to the economic growth and wellbeing of that Nation.

This practice is increasingly being embraced by governments of many countries through the introduction of incentives and special intervention programs that serves as a motivation for many potential businesses who eventually take advantage of these opportunities.

The features of this new approach include:

1. The provision of support, encouragement and development of small and medium businesses through various government policies and incentives.

2. The recruitment of highly skilled and educated workforce to aid in the improvement and expansion of infrastructure for these small establishments.

These approaches are targeted at creating an attractive business climate and improving the quality of life of the immediate community. Similarly, since job creation is one of the key objectives of economic growth, creating a conducive environment for small and medium businesses is likely to help them experience rapid growth and produce more jobs for the local community from several small and medium businesses than one single large business enterprise (Edmiston 2007).

Some incentives introduced in some Countries

During the development of this book, we conducted a survey of some small and medium businesses to find out what incentives the government has provided for them. The survey results revealed that the government put in place some special intervention programs which they tapped into that provided them with incentives that has helped them start and grow their businesses. Based on the survey results, the government incentives to start new businesses or grow existing ones include:

- The provision of training, orientation, coaching, mentoring and capacity building for the owners and members of staff of the small and medium business

- The provision of funds to start their businesses

- The provision of funds for the growth and expansion of the businesses

- The provision of equipment's for their business

- The provision of infrastructure and power for the business

To further buttress the importance of small and medium businesses in the growth of the economy of a nation, research has shown that these businesses help in the following ways:

- They help in meeting the needs of the locals where ever they are located

- They serve as a very important source of employment

- They help motivate the population and provide success stories for the future generation

- Small businesses are flexible and can more easily respond more flexibly to the challenges and problems in any community compared to larger business

- Small businesses are much more situated to building one on one closer relationship with their clients, suppliers and employees like wise.

- They help individuals generate their own income, revenue and profits making you earn more money which will relatively add to the GDP of the country

- Businesses also create wealth to the individual and increase capital in the community in the nation as a whole.

- Working for others makes you vulnerable to redundancy and idleness, closures or mergers as such your own business helps you plan for your own future, crates independence for the individual or group, gives you the opportunity to be your own boss such that you can choose your own working hours.

- It brings out hidden talents of individuals and work from home

- Small businesses makes it more easier to responds to new competition, trends and other developments in the community

- In rapid shifting markets and saturated markets, consumers view innovation and new business ideas as aspects that adds value to companies, products, goods and services. If this strategy is properly planned and developed, it can be used to develop a unique selling point to attract more customers leading to explosive growth of the business and bring in revenue to the state.

- Since the business environment is very dynamic, smaller businesses can more easily introduce new ideas that can be more difficult or take more time to introduce to in larger businesses. The success of these innovations these days usually attract interest by larger businesses and are often bought off by larger businesses. The list goes on and on.

The connect

Businesses are usually initiated by internal business needs or external influences, these needs in most cases trigger or set off the creation of a feasibility study, a need analysis, or even a description of what the business will address. This business need may also be based on a market demand, technological advancement, legal requirement or changes in government regulation.

As seen earlier in this book, Urban agglomerations is increasing globally in an alarming rate, and with half of the world's population now living in urban areas, the future population is expected to be absorbed by the urban areas be it small or large.

The challenging task of managing urban areas with this increase in population in both Urban and rural areas has increased and will continue to increase over time in both scope and complexity. This will considerably increase the pressure of infrastructure, and other basic amenities hence the need for creative business initiatives (reflecting these in new patterns) to address these impending problems in the 21st century.

In order to help you develop creative business initiatives to address these impending problems in the 21st century, this book highlights innovative and strategic approaches used by professionals via a multidisciplinary approach to equip the reader in order to help them organise knowledge so that they can intelligently direct it through a number of problem solving techniques and the creation of practical plans of actions to the definite end of accumulation of wealth. The book also explores available opportunities like the establishment of your own business, growing your existing business or even putting together initiatives in which ever company or organisation you work, to help you optimise your working environment and processes for better products, service delivery, customer satisfaction and profit for the organisation.

The subsequent part of this book is focused on impacting knowledge on what the reader should know and do in other to develop ideas to start up a new business, grow and optimise performance of an existing one with the sole aim of developing a successful venture.

Chapter Two: The Starting point

The objective of this topic is to throw more light on one of the core areas of concern in starting your own business. Here we look at the first steps required to be taken in this endeavour and the logical approach to one of the greatest tools used in business known to mankind. Furthermore, we apply a number of steps used in systematic problem solving. This is because you want to ensure that the solutions that are being developed are factual, objective and realistic.

Rules for developing a successful business

Just as we have different kinds of businesses and different factors affecting them, we also have different rules required to achieve success in the different types of business. It should be understood that no one rule fits all business, as such, thorough research needs to be carried out on the industry you choose so that you can understand the basic principles obtainable there. However, based on research and the survey data obtained during the development of this book, there are some basic rules that successful businesses have applied in the past that have helped them record high levels of success in their venture. These include:

- Successful business owners ensure that they work hard and Smart in order to achieve success

- Successful business owners ensures that all members of the team he develops work together as a team and celebrate success recorded by each member of the team.

- In order to be successful, you must ensure that you have actually found a need and that your business is actually providing the solution adequately and as effectively and efficiently as possible for full customer/client satisfaction

- Successful business owners ensure that he or she is committed to the work

- Successful business owners understand that it is their responsibility to ensure the staff are motivated to carry out their tasks

- Successful business owners ensure that there is good communications across all levels of management in the business

- Successful business owners ensures that proper appreciation should be accorded to any member of the team that performs well

- Successful business owners ensures that they set achievable goals

Pre start-up mind-set

Investments to be made

A typical approach to starting a business requires that the first types of investments to be made include intellectual investments, Physical investment and Emotional investment.

The Intellectual investment refers to the hours spent to create and refine your research work.

Physical investment refers to the time and hours that will be spent in making your presentation research and gathering resources.

Emotional investment refers to the time/hours spent in thinking about what the business can do for you, your family, your career, etc.

It is important to invest quality time on these areas as this will go a long way in guiding and supporting the decisions you make.

Business risks

The English dictionary defines risk as the possibility that something bad or unpleasant will happen. In starting up a business, it is important that the initiator carries a positive mind set believing that everything will work out well and as he/she planned. However, it is very important that the owner plans for uncertainty.

Planning risk management refers to the processes comprising of identifying and analysing possible risks that may impact the business and also planning adequate responses such that when these risk surface in the course of the development stages, there are already pre-planned measures in place to mitigate the negative impacts. That said, the objective of this is mainly to increase the likelihood and positive events at the same time reducing those negative ones occurring. As we proceed in this book, we will further explain how to identify and analyse the risks that may impact your business.

Naming the business

Some researchers consider this a very important aspect as you don't want to name a business today only to find out a couple of months or years later that you have given the business a wrong name and want to change it. Ample time should be taking to carefully develop names that will suit the business. It is also worthy of note to have two or three names on standby when going to register the business with the authorised government agency in your location. It is also worthy of note that your business name has distinctive as well as descriptive elements, A distinctive element will be something like XYZ while a descriptive element will be something like facility managers, bakery, real estate, energy, environmental services, photography, etc.

Personal questions you need to answer

To enable them make the right decisions at the early stages, survey data obtained during the development of this book revealed that, successful business owners had to provide answers to questions like:

- Why am I starting the business and what kind of business do I want to do?

- Who are my target customers and what kind of products or services am I going to offer?

- What value is my business, product or service going to add to my target customers and is it going to be worth the stress?

- Am I willing and prepared to spend time and money to get this business started?

- How can I make my own product or service different from what is currently obtained in the market?

- How do I intend to manage the business?

- How am I going to advertise the business?

- How long do I have to wait before I start making profit?

- Do I have an existing record keeping and accounting system? If not, how do I setup one?

- How and where do I know where to get professional advice and support from?

If you are having difficulty providing realistic answers to questions like these, the subsequent sections of this book will introduce you to approaches and techniques professionals have applied to start-ups that have provided and suitable answers and recorded brilliant successes.

Starting up

Successful business owners will tell you that starting up a business is about identifying a need and developing solutions to meet that need. Professionals call this problem solving.

As seen in previous sections of this book, business is about finding solutions to customer problems. A good business man or woman must be able to effectively solve his or her customer problems or provide solutions to their needs. For this reason, we will take a look at, how anyone can get good ideas to help you decide what you want to do, how to solve problems and problem solving strategies.

How to get good ideas

If an individual is to succeed in this endeavour, that person has to have good ideas. The concept of getting good ideas does not stop there, it is their personal responsibility to work on these good ideas to make them even better. This begins with active listening, being open minded and most importantly developing the willingness to listen to ideas of different people from different levels in life i.e. without prejudice to race, age, gender or even the amount of wealth possessed by the individual.

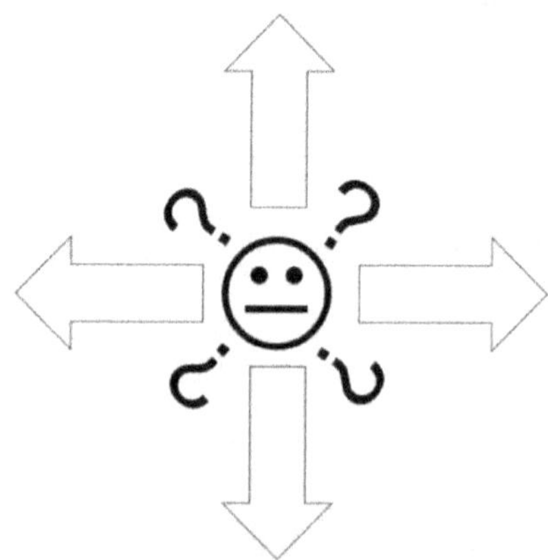

Not knowing what to do is a problem a lot of people face in trying to start a business. There are several ways of getting ideas that you can develop. First of all, you must understand that starting up a business is not rocket science. There are simple steps one can use. You must **decide what you want to do**. If you do not already know what you want to do, here are some strategic approaches to help you decide.

It should be noted that there are some things you don't want to hold you down for example, you may be worried that you have to create something so unique that no one has ever thought about. Such notions can pretty much weigh you down as its quite difficult getting something entirely new that no other person has ever worked on. Some analyst even consider this a big waste of time and resources.

Optimising existing ideas, businesses, products or services

This strategic approach used in generating ideas has been in in use for many years now. In deciding what you want to do, the thoughts and questions you should consider asking yourself should be things like:

- What ways can I possibly improve on this idea, business, product or service?

- Can I possibly do this better?

- Can I do it a little differently or advanced than what these other people are already doing?

- Can I make the process operate more simply, efficiently or even more effectively?

For example, you can study an idea, add innovation plus your own concept, customise it over and over again until you get something new with added functionality that will work better than the existing one and provide the much needed solution in your community.

This exercise was carried out by a couple of our volunteers during the research phase of this book. These individuals were grouped into four groups and below were the results of the ideas and business solutions some of the volunteers were able to draw out from their individual practical.

Group A	Group B
1. Business incubator 2. Setting up a call centre 3. Laundry business 4. Sales and training of security dogs	1. Coffee production 2. Food delivery service 3. Poultry 4. Provision of Nanny Service
Group C	**Group D**
1. Event Management and Party Planner 2. Cosmetic sales with home delivery service 3. Make-up Artistry 4. Content developer	1. CV/Resume Writing service 2. Telephone Answering service 3. Tour Guide and Travel Agency 4. Scholarship and Overseas Study consultant

Strategic approach using the mind mapping tool

The mind mapping tool is another strategic approach used in generating ideas. This strategy involves carrying out a series of tasks. Here, you do not have to over think it, rather, you just write down your thoughts. The aim is to develop the idea as less stressful as possible using the steps below.

1. Take a sheet of paper. At the centre of the sheet, write the words "start here", and in bracket write "me" and draw a circle around it.

2. Now draw another circle (above left hand side) and write down 10 things you feel you are very good at or things you derive pleasure and like to do. E.g. I like drawing, I like writing, I like cooking, I like working with my computer, I like developing solutions for companies etc. link it to the first circle in the middle of the paper

3. Next draw another circle (above right hand side) and write down 10 things you don't like to do or things you know or feel you are not good at doing. E.g. I don't like monotonous work, I don't like doing house chores, I don't like entering data, etc. link it to the first circle in the middle of the paper

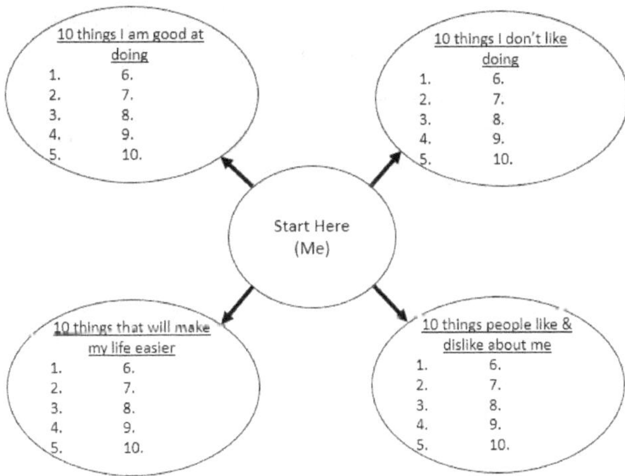

4. Next draw another circle (below left hand side) and write down 10 idea, business, product or service that you believe will make your easier, more efficient and effective, pleased etc. based on your previously written likes and dislikes. Circle it and link it to the first circle in the middle of the paper. Here you are considering yourself as a parent, employee, student, employer, business owner, buyer or seller etc.

5. Next examine your personal and professional life carefully and draw another circle (below right hand side) and write down 10 things about what you like or dislike about your personal and professional life and what you feel people like or dislike about you (i.e. about your character and personality). Link it to the first circle in the middle of the paper

6. Lastly, ask yourself why you think you want to start a business carefully studying all what you have written so far considering whether there is the need doing the things you

like to do. Critically analyse your whole write-up and you will eventually discover a pattern that will give you the proverbial light bulb telling you a list of ideas and things you would **want to do** (i.e. idea, business, product or service).

This exercise was carried out by a couple of our volunteers during the research phase of this book. These individuals were grouped into four groups and below were the results of the ideas and business solutions some of the volunteers were able to draw out from their individual practical.

Group A	Group B
1. Bottle water 2. Building and Construction 3. Mobil phone repairs 4. Leather Shoe Production	1. Metal Fabrication 2. Poultry 3. Engineering, Information and Communications (EIC) 4. Website design
Group C	**Group D**
1. Fashion& Design 2. Fish feed production 3. Maze farming 4. Paint Production	1. Glass cutting 2. Laundry services 3. Bakery/Food and Beverages 4. Automobile Mechanic

Strategic approach using the Time management Matrix

The Time management Matrix is another strategic approach that can be used in generating ideas. This strategy involves carrying out a series of tasks. Here, you also do not have to over think it, rather, you just write down your thoughts. The aim is to develop the idea as less stressful as possible using the steps below.

- Make a list of activities you have been engaged in the past one month

- Make a list of activities you are currently engaged in and those you hope to achieve in the next one month

- Develop a four (4) quadrant table as seen below labelling them urgent, not urgent, important and not important

	Urgent	Not Urgent
Important	Urgent/ Important: Pressing challenges, ad-hoc work from your boss, etc. 1. 2. 3. 4. 5.	Not urgent/ important: planning activities, kaizen activities, personal and professional development, mentoring, long term important goals etc. 1. 2. 3. 4. 5.
Not Important	Urgent/ Not important: Meetings that are not very important, unimportant reports, low priority phone calls, SMS, email, chatting, unnecessary interruptions, etc. 1. 2. 3. 4. 5.	Not urgent/ Not important: gossip at the work place, irrelevant and unimportant internet browsing, time wasting activities, etc. 1. 2. 3. 4. 5.

- Rearrange the list of activities into this table accordingly

  o Ensure that the activities on the not urgent but important section of the table

- Rank these activities according to high, medium and low categories

- Now focus your attention on the not urgent but important activities and look for a pattern to develop business solutions from this quadrant.

All of the above mentioned strategies can be used to generate ideas. However, this is only the first step in the endeavour as these ideas have to be further developed to ensure that the solutions are factual, objective and realistic. This can be achieved by systematic integration of the ideas with the Problem Solving tool for further development.

Developing ideas using Problem solving and problem solving strategies

The Problem Solving Tool is one of the greatest tools known to mankind that has been used by successful businesses, professionals and industry experts over the years. It can be defined as the system that uses generic or adhoc methods in an orderly manner to find solutions to problems. It may also be defined as the process of walking through the details of a problem in order to reach a solution. The strategies involved in problem solving include the act of defining a problem; determining the cause of the problem; identifying, prioritizing and selecting alternatives for a solution; and implementing a solution. The steps involved in problem solving can be seen in the figure below.

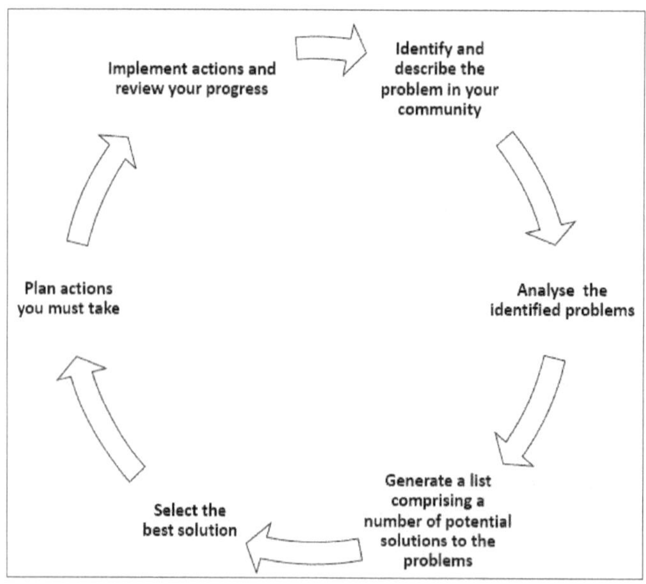

Figure 7: Problem solving

As seen in the figure above, the problem solving involves the following steps:

1. Identify and describe the problem in your community

2. Analyse the identified problems

3. Generate a list comprising a number of potential solutions to the problems

4. Analyse, evaluate your list of available options and select their best option

5. Put together a strategy and an action plan

6. Implement the most preferred option then monitor its development to be sure it really solves the problem

Step 1: Identify and describe the problem in your community

In other to identify and describe the problem in your community, the individual must be prepared to go the extra mile while looking into the immediate community where you are considering setting up the business. As earlier mentioned, this can be achieved by the systematic integration of the problem solving tool and any of the above mentioned strategic approaches (i.e. the Strategic approach using the mind mapping tool, the Time management Matrix or even optimising existing ideas, businesses, products or services).

However, in this section, we will be looking at another strategic approach that has been used by successful businesses, professionals and industry experts called the **gap analysis tool.**

Where I am	Gap	Where I want to be
• Frequent power failure in my immediate community		• I need constant power supply for me and my neighbours

Figure 8: Gap analysis tool

The figure above depicts a typical gap analysis tool. As seen in the figure, in order to identify and describe the problem in your community, you use the gap analysis tool. This can be achieved by drawing a table and writing out your current state. You then leave a gap in-between as seen in the figure above. You then write out the future state where you will like to be and then compare them

Where I am	Gap	Where I want to be
• Frequent power failure in my immediate community	• Start up a sales, supply and installation of solar panel business • Start up a sales, supply and installation of wind turbine business • Start up a sales, supply and installation of inverter business • Start up a sales, supply and installation of wind turbine business • Start up a sales, supply and installation of mini hydro power business • Start up a sales, supply and installation of biogas business	• I need constant power supply for me and my neighbours

Figure: the Gap analysis tool

If this is properly done, you realise that the gap in-between reveals numerous opportunities you may have never imagined ever existed. It is worthy of note that selection of gap filters should be as a result of thinking outside the box rather than business as usual. In the figure above, there are dozens of things that one can fill in the gap in-between them.

This tool has been proven to be very useful, not only for generating ideas for starting up new businesses, but also used by individuals working in medium and large companies and organisations to identify problems in the daily operations or other important activities.

It is also important to have in mind that when using these tools, the user should try as much as possible to integrate and develop these solutions based on challenges facing other businesses and external influences. This is because, research has shown that businesses which are born out of challenges facing other businesses and external influences are usually good for start-up businesses as they are known to have recorded higher success rates in the past. These challenges include things like increase in market demand, government regulations, economic policies, technological advancement, legal requirements etc.

Hands on

Now, take a good look at the immediate community where you live or work and use the gap analysis tool below to identify gaps under the following headings.

NB: If your business or work does not already have one, you can use this book to serve you as a guide to developing a gap analysis tool template for your business or organisation where you work. Feel free to reproduce the table and reuse it over and over and over.

Now populate the gap analyses table below based on challenges that may be as a result of increase in **market demand** in your community?

S/No	Where I am	Gap	Where I want to be
1			
2			
3			
4			
5			

Populate the gap analyses table below based on challenges that may be as a result of changes in **government regulations** in your community?

S/No	Where I am	Gap	Where I want to be
1			
2			
3			
4			
5			

Populate the gap analyses table below based on challenges that may be as a result of changes in **economic policies** in your Country?

S/No	Where I am	Gap	Where I want to be
1			
2			
3			
4			
5			

Populate the gap analyses table below based on challenges that may be as a result of changes in **technological advancement** in your community?

S/No	Where I am	Gap	Where I want to be
1			
2			
3			
4			
5			

Populate the gap analyses table below based on challenges that may be as a result of changes in **legal requirements** in your community?

S/No	Where I am	Gap	Where I want to be
1			
2			
3			
4			
5			

Step 2: Analyse the identified problems

After the problem has been identified (Step 1), the next step is to analyse this problem. The reason for this is to unravel the **main causes of the problem** to enable us develop sustainable solutions to the problem. A popular tool used by successful businesses, professionals and industry experts is the Root Cause Analysis (RCA) Tool. This system uses different strategic approaches to uncover causes of problems. Here, the identified problem is placed at the starting point of the diagram. Different causes of the problem are then linked, one after the other, to the problem in order to identify possible causes. In this case, you keep asking why until you identify the root cause of the problem.

The figure below shows how you make use of the cause and effect diagram to dig deeper to find out the causes of the problem.

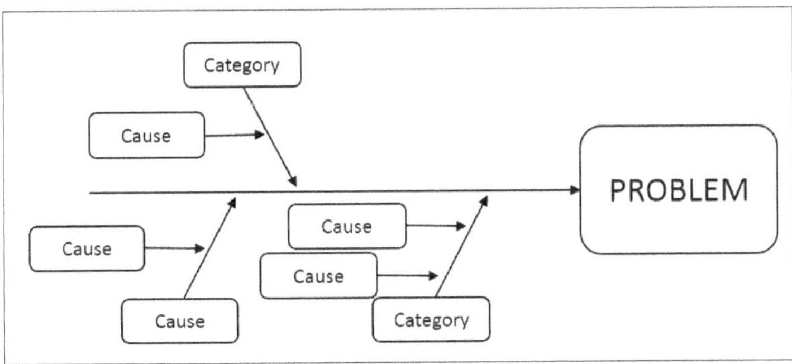

Figure 9: Root Cause Analysis (RCA) Tool

As seen in the figure above, the identified problem is placed at the extreme right hand side. The causes of the problem are then categorised and placed at the left hand side as seen in the figure above.

For example, you have identified a problem in your community which is: No commercial Business Centre (Internet café, document typesetting, photocopy, printing and scanning) within your local community. You have also done some investigations to find out that people living there (including yourself) waste time and spend a lot of money driving down to the nearest business centre which is about 5km away just to have access to these services. Use this RCA tool below to analyse the problem to ascertain the underlying causes of the problem.

NB: Do not over think it, just write it as the thought comes to your mind. If you feel you are not getting it right, you can seek further clarification on the subject via the email provided at the end of the book.

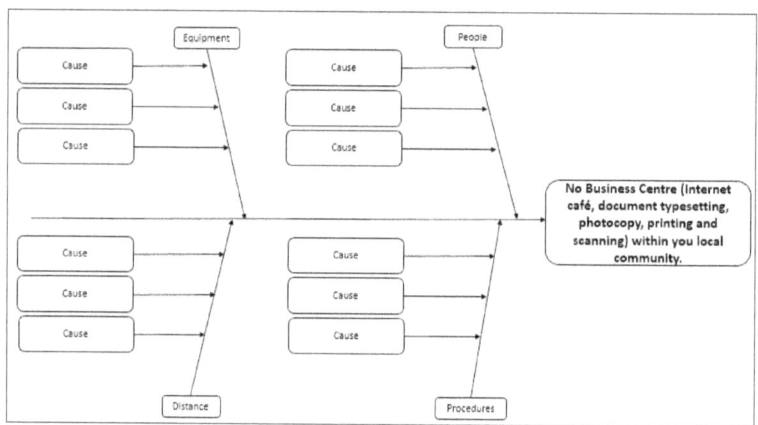

Hands on

Now, take a good look at the immediate community where you live or work and use Cause and effect tool below to investigate and populate the cause and effects tool under the following headings:

Challenges that may be as a result of **increase in market demand** in your community

Challenges that may be as a result of changes in **government regulations** in your community

Challenges that may be as a result of changes in **economic policies** in your Country?

Challenges that may be as a result of changes in **technological advancement** in your community

Challenges that may be as a result of changes in **legal requirements** in your community

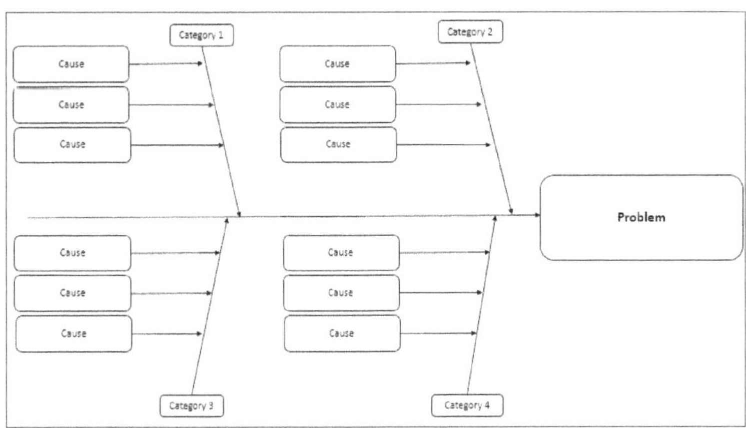

Step 3: Generate a list comprising a number of potential solutions to the problems

The next step involves generating a list of possible solutions to the underlying causes of the problem.

In this section, you need to apply various information gathering techniques to achieve your goal. Some information gathering techniques include group discussions, brainstorming and interviewing technique. It is very important that you take notes and record the list of generated ideas (solutions) during this section of your work. To help you get a broader view, you may need to seek support from a friend whom you feel may be interested in helping you out, an expert in your field or your mentor. This is to enable your generate unbiased results that are more factual and as realistic as possible.

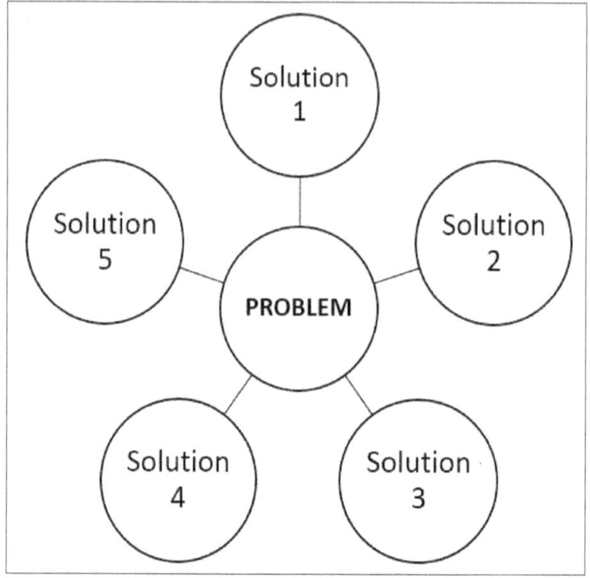

For example, you have identified that the problem you are trying to address is the challenge of poor power supply in your area. In order to convert this problem into business opportunity, you have put together several solutions via the use of group discussions, brainstorming sessions and interviewing technique. Below are the list generated:

- Start up a sales, supply and installation of solar panel business

- Start up a sales, supply and installation of wind turbine business

- Start up a sales, supply and installation of inverter business

- Start up a sales, supply and installation of wind turbine business

- Start up a sales, supply and installation of mini hydro power business

- Start up a sales, supply and installation of biogas business

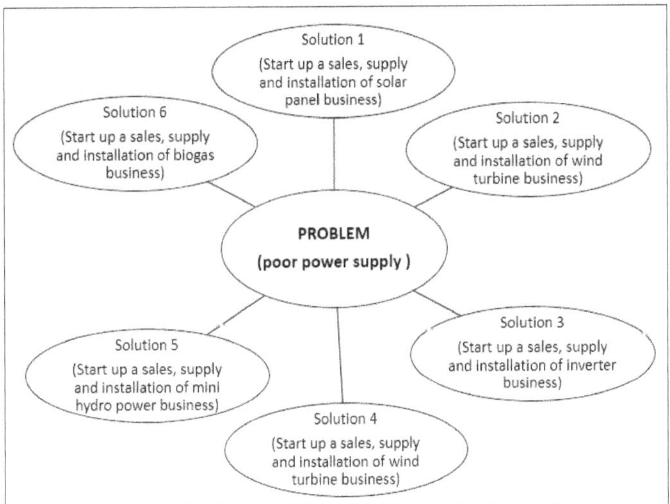

Hands on

Now, take a good look at the immediate environment where you live or work and use the group discussions, brainstorming sessions and interviewing technique to investigate and populate the tool with solutions under the following headings:

- Solutions to challenges that may be as a result of increase in **market demand** in your community

- Solutions to challenges that may be as a result of changes in **government regulations** in your community

- Solutions to challenges that may be as a result of changes in **economic policies** in your Country?

- Solutions to challenges that may be as a result of changes in **technological advancement** in your community

- Solutions to challenges that may be as a result of changes in **legal requirements** in your community

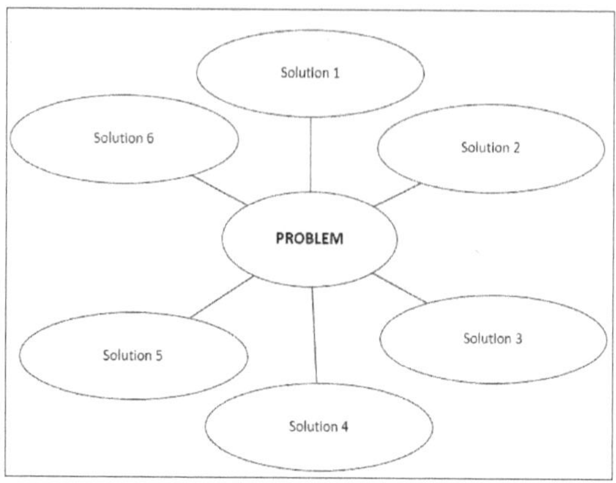

Step 4: Analyse and evaluate your list of available options to select the best option

The next step involves doing some evaluation on the list of generated solutions in order identify which one will be most preferred to choose and develop further.

Thorough decision analysis is of critical importance in selecting a preferred option from a list of identified solutions since we know that initiatives that follow good system, processes usually consider several alternatives.

In this section of the work, it is required that you select the most favourable options to you I.e. Come up with an idea from the list and pick an idea that best fits your passions, goals, strengths, resources, and tolerance for risk. But keep in mind that your initial idea is just a hypothesis. Don't fall in love with it just yet. Remember, it's better to measure nine times and cut once than to measure once and cut nine times.

A popular tool used by decision makers in such situations is the **Multi-Criteria Decision Analysis tool** otherwise called the MCDA. It can be described as a decision analysis tool which can be used to help **business owners**, decision makers, **consultants,**

regulators make decisions when given a list of multiple and complex options.

<u>Steps in carrying out MCDA</u>

Objective strategies for choosing an applicable MCDA method are rare. However, the stages in using the MCDA include:

1. Identify and define the problem

2. Identify stakeholders: *e.g. The Business owner and what they are really looking for in the business*

3. Identify the available options e.g. *Office locations in Aberdeen, Dundee and Edinburgh*

4. Identify criteria *e.g. Rent, electricity, cleaning, rest cost, office size, quality of working conditions*

5. Assign weights to the criteria and test for suitability:

    a. **Weights i:** Assign **weights** to the criteria

    b. **Weights ii:** Determine **weights** to each criteria

6. Carry out the analysis

7. Perform sensitivity analysis *i.e. to see how robust the decision responds to changes in the figures supplied by the owner; you manipulate/ play around with the figures*

8. Draw your conclusion

Example:

Now, back to the list of available solutions to addressing power problems in our initial example. Let's use the MCDA tool to analyse the list of available options.

1. Identify and define the problem

    a. *Power failure*

2. Identify stakeholders: *e.g. The Business owner and what they are really looking for in the business*

    a. *You*

3. Identify the available options

    a. *Start up a sales, supply and installation of solar panel business*

    b. *Start up a sales, supply and installation of wind turbine business*

    c. *Start up a sales, supply and installation of inverter business*

    d. *Start up a sales, supply and installation of mini hydro power business*

    e. *Start up a sales, supply and installation of biogas business*

4. Identify criteria

    a. *Rent, start-up cost, acceptability, availability, reliability and risk*

5. Assign weights to the criteria and test for suitability:

    a. **Weights i:** Assign **weights** to the criteria

    b. **Weights ii:** Determine **weights** to each criteria

        i. *Rent (3), start-up cost (3), acceptability(2), availability(3), reliability(3) and risk (2)*

6. Carry out the analysis

    a. *Populate the table and carry out evaluation*

	Criteria 1		Criteria 2		Criteria 3		Criteria 4		Criteria 5		Criteria 6		Overall score
Solutions	Rent		Start-up Cost		Acceptability		Availability		Reliability		Risk		
Start up a sales, supply and installation of solar panel business	5(15)	15	5(15)	15	3(8)	8	5(15)	15	4(12)	12	5(10)	10	75
Start up a sales, supply and installation of wind turbine business	4(3)	3	4(12)	12	3(6)	6	4(12)	12	4(9)	9	2(4)	4	46
Start up a sales, supply and installation of inverter business	5(15)	15	5(15)	15	4(8)	8	4(12)	12	4(12)	12	2(4)	4	66
Start up a sales, supply and installation of mini hydro power business	3(9)	9	3(9)	9	3(6)	6	4(12)	12	4(12)	12	2(2)	2	50
Start up a sales, supply and installation of biogas business	3(9)	9	3(6)	6	3(6)	6	5(15)	15	5(15)	15	2(4)	4	55
Weighing criteria	3		3		2		3		3		2		
Scale from 1: Least preferred – 5: most preferred													

7. Perform sensitivity analysis *i.e. to see how robust the decision responds to changes in the figures supplied by the owner; you manipulate/ play around with the figures*

   a. *Optional*

8. Draw your conclusion

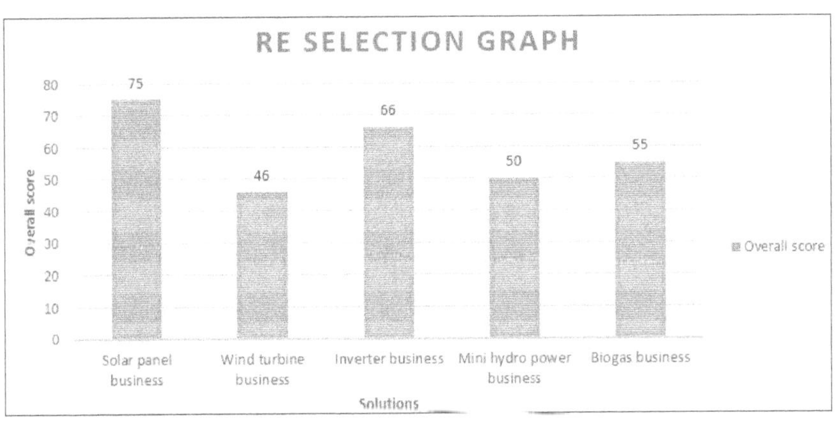

From the analysis carried out, it can be seen that this system has enabled us compare each solution side by side and the solution with the highest overall score is the Solar panel option. It is this option that will be considered the favourable option that will then be developed further in the next phase.

This system can be used in different ways and its usage is not limited to the criteria used in this example.

Though this tool is a strong decision support tool used by many professionals in making sound decisions, care should be taking when using it as though it has strengths, it also has some limitations.

Strengths

- This approach has the advantage of providing reliable results that are used in decision making.

- The approach usually provides for all 3 sustainability considerations e.g. Society, environment and Economic considerations.

Limitations

MCDA is considered to be a very active field of research as it has a lot of applications. However, it is considered to have some limitations. These include:

- Personal interest may affect choice and weighing of the indicators/Criteria

- Social indicators/criteria may not be properly justified using figures to weigh them

- Population increase

- Inflation rate

- Data may not be accurate

- People tend to lie for obvious reasons regarding decisions to be taken

- Stakeholder satisfaction

- Limited budgets

- Tight deadlines

- Interpretation

Effectiveness of MCDA

- It is better than doing nothing

- It is a Systematic decision support tool

- It gives you more information in making your decision

Hands on

Now, from the solutions you have developed in the previous sections (your personal solutions), make use the sample table below to carry out MCDA. Assign weights (where appropriate) to the criteria you wish to use and arrive at the solution with the highest value.

	Criteria 1		Criteria 2		Criteria 3		Criteria 4		Criteria 5		Criteria 6		Overall score
Solutions													
Start up a sales, supply and installation of solar panel business													
Start up a sales, supply and installation of wind turbine business													
Start up a sales, supply and installation of inverter business													
Start up a sales, supply and installation of mini hydro power business													
Start up a sales, supply and installation of biogas business													
Weighing criteria													
Scale from 1: Least preferred – 5: most preferred													

Put together a strategy and an action plan

The next thing to do is to put together your action plan. **Action planning** can be defined as the process that is meant to help you focus your business ideas and decide what strategy or steps you need to take(within a given time) in order to achieve the goals you have set out for yourself. This may also means that you state all actions required to achieve success, write out the cost of implementing them and contingency arrangements put in place.

You should document this information and ensure that you have alternative plans. A timeframe should be attached on this area.

	Activity	Resources required	Roles and responsibilities	Time	Status	Comments
	Here, the idea is to make a list of the activities tasks you intend to carry out using your chosen methods over a particular period of time	Here, the idea is to make a list of resources that will be needed for your activities tasks	Here, the idea is to allocate individuals with tasks and activities and their associated resource requirements	Here, the idea I to attach a time line to all activities and tasks meant to be carried out.	Here, the idea is identify if the task is completed of not complete.	Here, the idea is meant to record what happened, what you learnt in the process and note how you can improve on it next time.
1						
2						
3						
4						

Figure 10: Action planning tool

As seen in the figure above, the action plan tool depicts where you get your planned activities written down, what you need to do and the dates your intend completing the tasks. You need to ensure that you organise your actions across the timeline. This timeline is important because it helps you organise your activities so that they do not clash.

For example, you want to develop a website for some unique business idea, you have successfully carried out previous analysis and come to the conclusion that the website you are considering developing will be a profitable venture. Let's look at a sample action plan below.

	Activity	Resources required	Roles and responsibilities	Time	Status	Comments
1	Choose a business name, domain name and trademark if possible. You should also check if the names chosen are available, if not, choses another one	$--	• Mr Smith Roy • Mr Brown Joe • Mrs Susan Pascal	---days		
2	Develop the structure of the business you hope to start	$--	• Mr Smith Roy • Mr Brown Joe • Mrs Susan Pascal	---days		
3	Conduct market research	$--	• Mr Smith Roy • Mr John Bryan	---days		
4	Develop business plan	$--	• Mr Smith Roy • Mrs Susan Pascal • Allen Solomon	---days		
5	Develop marketing plan	$--	• Mr Smith Roy • Mrs Susan Pascal • Allen Solomon	---days		
6	Find partners	$--	• Mr Smith Roy • Mrs Betty Andrew	---days		
7	Get funding	$--	• Mr Smith Roy • Mustapha Kazim	---days		
8	Design your logo	$--	• Mrs Adel Wilson • Mr Raymond Hill	---days		
9	Put together content for the website	$--	• Mr Smith Roy • Mrs Susan Pascal	---days		
10	Set up the website	$--	• Mr Raymond Hill • Albert Ezom	---days		
11	Setup your accounting system for the proposed website	$--	• Mr Brown Joe • Mrs Susan Pascal	---days		
12	Develop price list	$--	• Mr Raymond Hill • Albert Ezom • Mr Brown Joe • Mrs Susan Pascal	---days		
13	Run pilot test of the website	$--	• Mr Smith Roy • Mr Raymond Hill • Albert Ezom	---days		
14	Review the work done	$--	• All team members	---days		
15	Launch the website	$--	• Mr Smith Roy • Mr Brown Joe • Mrs Susan Pascal	---days		

Hands on

Now, from the solution you have identified as the most preferred from the previous stage (your personal solutions), use the action plan below to fill in the gaps and develop an action plan for this new business initiative.

	Activity	Resources required	Roles and responsibilities	Time	Status	Comments
1						
2						
3						
4						

Execution and monitoring

The idea here is to implement the most preferred option and monitor its development to be sure it really addresses the problem.

This step is iterative in nature and has to be closely monitored to ensure the plans are going on, as initially specified in the action plan. Things to avoid here are mind traps and process traps. However, it is important to give your goals priority and accept your mistakes as you progress in the work.

Investments are required to be made

- Intellectual investment: spend hours to crate and refine your research work

- Physical investment: spend time, hours making your presentation research and resources

- Emotional investment: thinking about what your business can do for you, your family, your career, etc.

To succeed in this endeavour, you have to develop good ideas and work on them to make them even better. It begins with open mindedness and willingness to listen to all ideas from people.

Never shut down good ideas as his may prevent good ones from coming in.

Embark on shared thinking as this in often better than thinking individually. The reason is that research has shown this to be faster, more innovative and of greater value than

- Never be too quick to dwell on a single idea

- Multitude of ideas, high creativity and unlimited opportunities create an outstanding potential for growth

- Be open to multitude of ides and options and if it does not work, replace it with another one and move ahead

- We should search for ideas /problems in unusual places. It is important to search for these ideas as they do not come looking for you.

You can search for ideas in newspapers, news, TV, radio, listen to people and your colleagues.

Hands on

Now, from the action plan you have developed, start implementation.

Chapter Three: Strategic approaches to conducting Market research

At the initial stage, before any individual will commit a considerable amount of their finances and other resources into a business venture, it is important that the individual takes he's or her time to thoroughly gather most recent and accurate information about the business, its nature, existing and prospective customers that will patronize the business. This data should be as accurate as possible because it is essential for the success of the business. The concept of embarking on this endeavour is called **Market Research (MR).**

Definition of Market research: this can be said to be the process embarking on a study on the past, present and potential customers for the good, product or service. It involves the collecting/gathering, evaluating, analysing and interpreting data about a market, goods, service or products that is meant to be introduced or put for sale in the market.

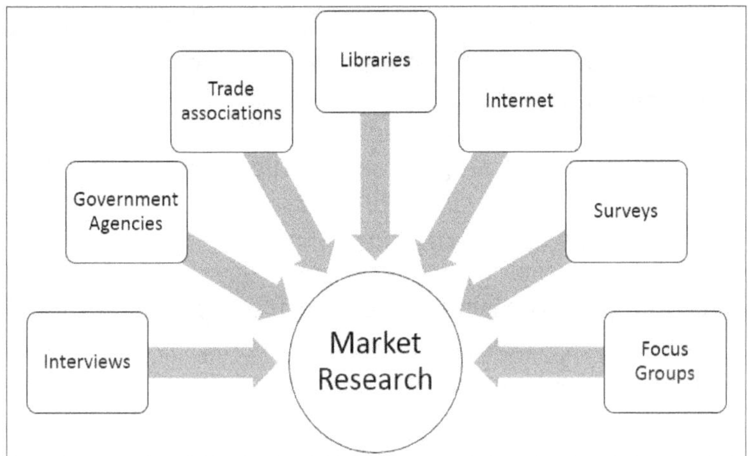

Other studies included in the market research are the investigation of the spending habits, business needs, location, target market and competitors you are likely to face in the business. All collated data are represented using tables, figures and diagrams. This information is then interpreted and documented for further action in achieving the business objectives.

Role of Market research

The role of conducting a market research in starting up a business cannot be over emphasized. It provides the entrepreneur or management with a more accurate and reliable data that will help them make better decisions in starting up the business. It gives the business owner or organisation a competitive edge in the industry as it is able to predict customer behaviour to a certain level.

Characteristics of Market research

- A typical market research is objective and systematic as such, systematic planning is required.

- The procedures followed at each stage in the market research are planned in advance. It is methodical and well documented.

- Market research should be conducted impartially since it attempts to make available a more accurate information that will reflect the true state of affairs.

- Market research should be free from personal or political biases of the researcher or the management as research which is motivated by personal gains is considered a breach of professional standards and conducts.

Advantages and disadvantages of Market research

This book makes numerous references to starting up a new business. However, the concept is designed to work for both new business as well as existing business in the verge of starting or introducing a new product or service into the market. Industry leaders also have a lot to benefit from this book as extensive research (performed correctly) is known to help industry giants stay ahead of their competitors.

Now we will take a closer look at the advantages and disadvantages of market research.

Advantages of Market research

As explained above, market research is very important in starting up a new business or introducing a new product or service (by an existing business). It helps in the following ways:

- It helps in reducing doubt and uncertainty: as we all know, research typically involves contributing to knowledge that already exists. It also gives us an insight of possible loopholes and opportunities that are available in the future. This will assist the decision maker make more accurate decisions.

- It helps the decision maker revaluate previous studies and plans already made.

Disadvantages of Market research

Market research is designed to study consumer behaviour and the market environment for that particular business. However, the business environment is dynamic and changes continually, as such, these factors keep on changing and cannot give the exact information.

- Market research is known to be a social science. So, it cannot give exact solutions.

- Market research may be somewhat expensive

- It may be time consuming

- It may have limited scope or even limited practical value

- The research may face resistance from managers or from other sectors, as such, the research may not produce accurate results or even predict accurate consumer behaviour

Developing a clearer understanding of the potential market

It is a clear understanding that the market is very dynamic and in order to stay ahead of your game, you have to learn to adopt new strategies integrated with most recent (and modern) tools and techniques into your business to make it a success. This book will equip and enable you organise newly acquired knowledge and skills so that you can intelligently direct it to achieve success in your endeavour.

Even if your business is an old one or a new one, it is important for you to understand that a lot of research work has already been done on businesses similar to yours. Meaning that you do not have start your market research on every single detail from scratch, rather, all you need to do is to start your research from other businesses similar to yours, making use of existing information you can lay your hands on and then proceed from there.

It is worthy to note that before you set up the new business venture or introduce a new product or service into the market, it is important that you put in a lot of time and effort to thoroughly research your market. This is Important because having deep knowledge of your potential customers and competitors can help you be more successful in the venture.

In this book, we explore a few tips on researching your potential market. To have a clearer understanding of your requirements, you can start by asking yourself these questions relating to the business idea, product or service.

- Who?

- What?

- Where?

- When?

- Why?

- How?

This can give you a start-up point. As you go along asking yourself these questions and providing answers to them, your vision gradually becomes clearer and you begin to have an idea of the direction you are heading. These questions can be systematically manipulated to reflect the particular potential market you are seeking to research. However, for the purpose of providing strategic approaches that may be used, we provide the following examples:

- The who identifies your potential customers

- The **what** identifies your potential product

- The **where** identifies your potential location

- The **when** refers to time

- The **why** identifies your propose for the business and why you need to do it

- The **how** refers to how you are going to go about it

After answering these questions, the next thing to do is to investigate whether this solution you have developed is actually meeting the need of the people.

- Is it worth it?

- Do you think people will be willing to pay for this service?

This time around, you need to actually meet and discuss with the people you feel will be making use of your product.

Strategic approaches for MR

The idea of market research is to gather relevant information that will be used to reach out to potential customers and proffer solutions to possible market problems which the business may likely meet along the line or in the future.

Some strategic approaches for Market research used by successful businesses include:

- Market segmentation

- Product differentiation

Some techniques for conducting market research include:

- Historical

- Experimental

- Observational or

- Survey method

Types of data collected during MR

The types of data collected during market research include:

- The Primary data

- The Secondary data

The Primary data: some examples include the information you gather by yourself or the type you pay people to collect and analyse for your business.

The Secondary data: Some examples include information already collected and assembled by some persons or group of persons and have been made available for others to access. In some instances, the information may be free and at other times you may have to pay for them. In their bid to accelerate Economic growth and development, Government of some countries invest a lot of money on research to compile such information for the population. This information is then published on various medium (like the internet) for free access to the public.

Places where you can find Secondary data include government agency websites, industry reports, competitors data, Trade associations, research from other companies.

Data collection methods

There are different data collection methods during the development of the MR. While simple methods include just asking questions, some professionals and industry experts dealing with larger organisations make use of a more complex technique like the Delphi technique. However, some strategic approaches used in data collection include:

- Data collection via Direct Mail

- Data collection via Phone Surveys

- Data collection via Personal Interviews

- Data collection via Questionnaire

- Data collection via Group discussions

- Data collection from the Public

- Data collection via Research

According to the Book the Discipline of Market Leaders, it explains that customers want more of the things that the value. If the value low cost, they want it even lower. If the value speed the want it a lot easier and faster. And if they value advanced technology, they want it pushed a step further. If you are going to research on your potential market in order to develop a deep knowledge of your potential customers, these and similar opportunities are likely areas you may want to explore. Bearing this in mind, you may want to:

- Choose customers

- Narrow your market

- Dominate your market

Factors affecting the use of market research information

One of the major challenges affecting the market research is the accuracy of the data collected. This mainly depends on a number of factors.

1. Sample size

2. Quota sample

3. Data type (Primary or secondary data)

4. Bias information

Sample size

The sample size refers to the amount of data collected during the research. If the data collected is from a relative small group, the results may not represent the larger population and data may be inaccurate and may produce wrong results. Thus, the larger the better.

Quota sample

For a better result, it is important that the data is randomly collected. If this is not the case, the data may only represent a particular group from the public and my likely produce inaccurate results.

Data type (Primary or secondary data)

Primary data is information you collected yourself while secondary data is the one collected from someone other persons findings. Primary data is more preferred for your research because you will not to have a more accurate results while secondary data may be bias. This may be as a result that the person who collected the data may have done this for personal reasons. However, some experts argue that a combination of both methods is likely to produce more accurate results. This choice is yours as you should be able to put your available resources into consideration before you determine the appropriate approach to use that will suite you.

Bias Information

By this, we mean data collected from sources like the newspaper TV and other similar sources. The information may represent the interest of the particular media or it may be that the statistics may have even been out dated as such may not be an accurate source for use in your market research.

Market research report

Market research data is very important in determining focus areas needed in the final determination of results for the business. These includes focus areas like market trends, competitive market forces, standard terms and conditions, industry capabilities and standards and also the availability of products or services.

Developers should ensure proper documentation of their findings in a way that will properly support most accurate decision making. Proper documentation of the market research enables you to adequately carry out effective and efficient analysis, preserves your records, minimizes duplication of efforts and enables proper sharing of information for effective communication. Research has shown that different companies make use of different topics and headlines in developing their market research reports. Below are possible topics that was used based on a sample prepared by Professor Stephan Sorger a marketing author.

MARKET RESEARCH REPORT

1. Product/Service required

    a. Slogan

    b. List of team members

2. Introduction

    a. Situation

    b. Problem Statement

    c. Research process

3. Research objectives

    a. Objectives

4. Method

Hands on

Now, from the solutions you have developed in the previous sections, use the Market Research questionnaire template below to carry out a market research on a business you have selected to research on. Feel free to populate, edit and reproduce the table as required. When completed, use it to develop a **Market research report** based on the topics given in the previous section.

Market Research questionnaire

Market Research Questionnaire			
Business name: Product/Service/Category: Business owner: Date:			
Prepared by:			
Product/Service/Category description:			
	Questions	**Options**	**Comments**
1	What is your overall perception of the Product/Service described above?	1. Poor 2. Fair 3. Neutral 4. Good 5. Excellent	
2	What do you like best about the product/service described above?		
3	What do you dislike about the product/service described above?		
4	In your opinion, what is the level of quality you can assign to the product/service?	1. Low Quality 2. Fair Quality 3. Neutral 4. Good Quality 5. High Quality	
5	What do you feel about this product/service described above?	1. No Value 2. little Value 3. average value 4. Good Value 5. Excellent Value	
6	What do you feel about the following features in the product/service described above? 1. Feature A 2. Feature B 3. Feature C	1. Not important 2. A bit important 3. Neutral 4. Important 5. Very important	
7	Can you rate the following features (from 1 to 5) in the product/service described above? 4. Feature A 5. Feature B 6. Feature C	1. Not important 2. A bit important 3. Neutral 4. Important 5. Very important	1. 2. 3. 4. 5.

8	If the product/service was available, would you be interested in purchasing the product or service?	1. Not Interested 2. A little bit interested 3. Neutral 4. Interested 5. Very Interested	
9	What will be your obvious reason for purchasing this product/service?		
10	What do you think about the current price of the product/service?		
11	If you were giving a discount on the product/services, would you be interested in purchasing it?	1. Not Interested 2. A little bit interested 3. Neutral 4. Interested 5. Very Interested	
12	If offered alternatives, would you select this product/service over the others?	• No • Yes	Please explain here:
13	Have you previously bought a similar product/service?	• No • Yes	
14	What would you say is the most important reason for purchasing this product/service? (Multiple choices can be made here)	1. High value 2. Top Performance 3. Brand name Recognition 4. High Quality 5. Convenience 6. Good price	Please explain here:
15	What age range do you fall within?	1. 18-30 2. 31-40 3. 41-50 4. Over 50	
16	What income range do you fall within?	1. Below $20, 000 2. $20, 000–30,000 3. $31, 000–40,000 4. $41, 000–50,000 5. Over $50,000	

Chapter Four: Strategic approaches to Planning and development

ersonal development planning (PDP)

Personal development planning can be described as the process involved in creating an action plan based on goal-setting, values, awareness, thinking, and planning for the purpose of personal development within the context of a career, business, education, relationship or for self-improvement. The purpose of a personal development plan is to help you organise your personal goals in other to make them achievable within a stipulated period of time.

PDP have been known to provide an exciting, flexible and very powerful means of linking people's personal and professional development with the development of your business. Research has shown that people who have previously developed personal development plan usually achieve a higher degree of success in their respective endeavours.

The idea is to develop and integrate your PDP in line with the business solution you have been working on in the previous sections of this book. Here, should be more concerned about continuous development and change based on the information you have found about your customer's needs from the market research conducted earlier on. The process is iterative in nature, because you are meant to address issues that arise from your previous market research, align your PDP with it and then go back to the drawing board to do more research and improve on your product/service until you are certain your customers will be willing to pay for the product of services. Care should be taken not to completely change the product entirely, rather, you should be willing to use innovation to creatively use your resources and skills in developing the perfect product or service.

Benefits of having a Personal development planning

The advantages of having a Personal development plan include:

- You become self-aware of the task you are currently engaged in

- You naturally become more motivated

- You become a better learner from your mistakes

- Gradually grow to become more aware of your potential

Stages of developing a PDP

Stage 1- Personal analysis: The first stage in developing your PDP is to carry out a comprehensive analysis of your strengths, weakness, opportunities and threats. You are to ensure that you try as much as you can to relate this analysis as closely linked to your business solution as possible. A typical tool used to carry out such analysis is the SWOT analysis tool. See example below.

	Helpful	Harmful
	Strengths	**Weakness**
Internal	1. 2. 3. 4. 5.	1. 2. 3. 4. 5.
	Opportunities	**Threats**
External	1. 2. 3. 4. 5.	1. 2. 3. 4. 5.

For your strengths, you should include things like:

- What are your strengths that you feel can and will greatly support your business solution?

  - *List them.*

- What do you feel you can do better than others?

  - *List them.*

- What unique capabilities and resources do you have that will greatly support your business solution?

  - *List them.*

- What do other people perceive as your strengths that will greatly support your business solution?

  - *List them.*

For your weaknesses, you should include things like:

- What are your weaknesses that you feel may negatively affect your new business solution?

- o *List them.*

- What do you feel your competitors can do better you?

  - o *List them.*

- What can you improve upon given your current situation?

  - o *List them.*

- What do other people perceive as your weaknesses that may negatively affect your new business solution?

  - o *List them.*

For opportunities, you should include things like:

- What trends of conditions in your present environment may positively impact on you or your new business solution?

  - o *List them.*

- What opportunities available to you and your new business solution?

  - o *List them.*

- For threats, you should include things like:

- What trends of conditions in your present environment may negatively impact on you or your new business solution?

  - o *List them.*

- What are your competitors currently doing that may impact on you or your new business solution?

  - o *List them.*

- What impacts do your weakness have on the threats to you?

  o *List them.*

- Do you consider your financial capabilities or support a threat to you or your new business solution?

Stage 2- Goals Setting: The second stage in developing your PDP is to set **SMART (Specific, Measurable, Achievable, Realistic and Time)** goals for yourself. Here, you will need to carry out a lot of consultation with more experienced professionals in the industry so that you can closely align your goals with the business solution. See example below.

What do I want to do?	What do I need to do?	What resources do I need to achieve success?	How do I measure success?	What are my target dates set for review?

Stage 3- Personal Objectives setting: The third stage in developing your PDP is to set out your personal objectives. This should be set in context of your business solution you have developed in the previous sections of this book. Research has shown that for better results, you should set it in three sections of single or multiple entries i.e. Short term, medium term and long term goals. See example below.

Short term goals (within the next 1 year)
1.
2.
3.
Medium term goals (within the next 2 – 4 years)
1.
2.
3.
Long term goals (after 3 years)
1.
2.
3.

Hands on

Now, develop a PDP (using all three stages) within the context of your business solution which you have developed from the previous sections of this book. Ensure you seek assistance from an industry expert in the field or industry related or most closely related to your business solution. Feel free to populate, edit and reproduce each sections in the templates as required.

My Personal Development Plan

Stage 1- Personal analysis:

<table>
<tr><td></td><td>Helpful</td><td>Harmful</td></tr>
<tr><td rowspan="6">Internal</td><td>Strengths</td><td>Weakness</td></tr>
<tr><td>1.</td><td>1.</td></tr>
<tr><td>2.</td><td>2.</td></tr>
<tr><td>3.</td><td>3.</td></tr>
<tr><td>4.</td><td>4.</td></tr>
<tr><td>5.</td><td>5.</td></tr>
<tr><td rowspan="6">External</td><td>Opportunities</td><td>Threats</td></tr>
<tr><td>1.</td><td>1.</td></tr>
<tr><td>2.</td><td>2.</td></tr>
<tr><td>3.</td><td>3.</td></tr>
<tr><td>4.</td><td>4.</td></tr>
<tr><td>5.</td><td>5.</td></tr>
</table>

Stage 2- Goals Setting:

What do I want to do?	What do I need to do?	What resources do I need to achieve success?	How do I measure success?	What are my target dates set for review?

Stage 3- Personal Objectives setting:

Short term goals (within the next 1 year)
1.
2.
3.
Medium term goals (within the next 2 – 4 years)
1.
2.
3.
Long term goals (after 3 years)
1.
2.
3.

After carrying out your market research and developing a PDP, the next strategic approach is to develop a business plan.

Develop the business plan

The business plan can be described as a document that provides an outline of your intended business, the strategy, the proposed market in which the business will operate and how it aims to be profitable. The idea of the business plan is also meant to give a brief overview of why your business will succeed when so many others have failed.

On the average, the business plan should be detailed enough to help you convince investors or other stakeholders of the value of your business since these people may be potential sources of funding for your business. As such, it should show some results from the market research you have previously carried out on your customers, sum up how you will meet the needs of customers and make profits at the same time.

A good business plan should be

- **Concise:** your business plan should have a simple summary of your business and its profitability strategy. By this, you should use very simple language when developing your business plan. The structure should also be simple rather than complex. This is important because you want your potential investors at a quick glance at your plan to understand the key important aspects of your business.

- **Specific**: you should be specific and the writing should be professionally done. This will help you illustrate how you wish to actually carry out your plan.

- You should have good **knowledge of your market**: if your business is going to succeed, having a good knowledge of your market is very vital to the success of the business. A part of your business plan should clearly provide details about your target market as this will go a long way at improving the quality of your business plan.

- **Knowledge of your finances**: a successful business is one that makes profit. You are required to be clear on financial matters as it is very important part of the business.

In developing a good business plan, it is important to embark on some little study on what and what needs to be considered and put in place if you are going to get it right. This can be seen in the next section.

Important things to do before you develop a business plan

There is a common say that "when you fail to plan, you are indirectly planning to fail".

In the world today, many business owners or would be business owners believe they only need a comprehensive business document like a business plan when they need to collect funds from a bank or an investor. This is not entirely true as developing the document for the purpose of getting funding can make you miss out on some very important issues that you may face latter in the business.

The business plan document is important for many other reasons like helping the individual, group or company identify strengths, weakness, opportunities and treats to the business. It will also serve as a road map to starting and developing the business. In addition, it is important to get an expert in the field review your document so you can be advised appropriately on amendments to the document as this will invariably increase the chances for recording success in your endeavour.

Below are some small but essential rough draft you are likely to make before actually starting to prepare the business plan document. These include:

1. Develop a simple business model using the business model canvas

2. Make a draft of the business purpose or justification,

3. Make SMART business objectives and related success criteria,

4. Make a list of High-level requirements,

5. Draft your assumptions and constraints,

6. Make high-level project description and boundaries,

7. Make a draft of High-level risks,

8. Make a brief summary of milestone and a schedule,

9. Make a summary budget for the business

10. Make a list of relevant stakeholders

11. Write out what constitutes success criteria

12. Make a draft for marketing plan

13. Develop the business project management plan

Develop a simple business model using the business model canvas

A business model can be said to be an abstract representation of your business solution while the business model canvas is a strategic tool that allows you innovate, design and develop your business model. This should be developed in order to give you a clearer picture of some areas that may otherwise appear sketchy in the development of your business plan.

Key partners	Key activities	Value proposition	Customer relationship	Customer segments
1. 2. 3. 4. 5.	1. 2. 3. 4. 5.	1. 2. 3. 4. 5	1. 2. 3. 4. 5.	1. 2. 3. 4. 5.
	Key resources 1. 2. 3. 4. 5.		Channels 1. 2. 3. 4. 5.	
Cost structure 1. 2. 3. 4. 5.			Revenue streams 1. 2. 3. 4. 5.	

Figure 11: Business model canvas

1. For the cost structure, you will be looking at things like: what important resources and activities are expensive and which ones are cheap, which one do you think best suites your model?

2. For your channels, you will be considering things like; what are the channels your customers expect you to reach them and how do you intend to reach them, what are the likely customer routes, which channels are most effective, efficient and cost effective?

3. For your customer relationship, your aim will be to integrate your customer relationship with your business

model. Here, you will be considering things like; what kind of relationship are your potential customers expecting you to establish with them and how do you intend to maintain these relationships. Which types of relationships have you already established and at what cost?

4. For your customer segments, you will be considering things like; what groups of people are we providing our solutions to and which segment are most important to us?

5. For your key activities, you will be considering things like; what are the activities that are important in successfully carrying out your plan, what are the likely customer relationships and their likely distribution channels?

6. For your key partners, you will be considering things like who are your important potential partners and suppliers, what are the likely resources you hope to acquire from them plus, what are the activities they are likely to provide to you?

7. For your key resources, you will be considering things like: what important resources do your business solution require for success, what are the likely distribution channels, what are the likely revenue streams?

8. For your revenue streams, you will be considering things like; what value are your customers currently paying and how are they currently paying, what value are they willing to pay and how do they prefer to pay, and what are the highest revenue generators in the business solution?

9. For your value propositions, you will be considering things like: what problems is your business solution likely to address and what value do you hope to deliver to your potential customers?

Make a draft of the business purpose or justification

This draft should constitute a brief description of what you believe is the purpose of the business, and if the business will be addressing any problems or fulfilling any needs, what are they? List them out.

Make a draft of the SMART business objectives

Developing a draft of the SMART (Specific, Measurable, Achievable, Realistic and Time) business objectives helps refining your proposed business plan before you even get started. By SMART business objectives, we mean that your business objectives should be:

- **Specific**: this means that you have to provide details of what needs to be done to achieve success

- **Measurable**: here, it means that the progress should be designed in such a way that it can be measured so that values can be attached to the progress

- **Achievable**: here we mean that the objectives have to be accepted by you 100%. If your objectives are not achievable, you might run into problems along the line. If you cannot guarantee success or achievability in your objectives, you might have to review your work and develop objectives that are achievable.

- **Realistic**: you need to ensure that your objectives are realistic. If they are not, you might as well be building a castle in the sky.

- **Time**: you need to have a time frame of achievement attached to the work you are doing. This has to be clearly started so having milestones such that you have an idea when you are spending too much time on one particular section of the business is very important.

Make a list of High-level requirements, business description and boundaries

Starting a business, as in initiating a project in project management requires defining high level requirements. In such instances, you then have to set boundaries around your business scope and then work within this boundary to further develop the proposed solution. By this, we mean:

- You set your scope boundaries

- Work within the scope

- Ensure you do not wonder outside this scope, but rather, you dig deeper into the business scope.

This level of the work is important as it helps you avoid unnecessary costs and ensures that your business outcome will be achieved. To further develop this high level requirements, you then make use of the progressive elaboration to expand on the high level requirements as more information become clearer to you.

Make a draft of risks to your Business Solution

Risk management is an extremely broad topic and we will only be discussing briefly on some highlights on making drafts of high level risks.

Risks can be said to be events that may happen that have potential negative or positive impacts on the business solution you are developing. While the negative impacts are referred to as threats and may cause harm to the success of your business solution being developed, the positive impacts may be referred to as opportunities that may benefit and help in the success of your business solution being developed.

Attempting to address every potential risks that may affect your business solution all at the same time may end up being a very costly, ineffective and time wasting venture using up a lot of valuable resources that may otherwise have been redirected for other more useful purposes.

The purpose of making a draft of high level risks is that it helps you identify which risks are likely to have the highest negative impacts on the success of your proposed business solution.

The first step is that you start by identifying the potential risks, next you perform qualitative risk analysis on these risks, perform quantitative risk analysis and then lastly, you plan risk responses based on the results.

Stage 1: Identifying risks

This process involves identifying and making a list of potential risks that are likely to have an impact on the success of your proposed business solutions objectives. One reliable tool used by professionals in identifying the risks is the SWOT analysis tool.

		Helpful	Harmful
		Strengths	**Weakness**
Internal		1. 2. 3. 4. 5.	1. 2. 3. 4. 5.
		Opportunities	**Threats**
External		1. 2. 3. 4. 5.	1. 2. 3. 4. 5.

Figure 12: Swot analysis tool

The use of this tool in identifying risks should be iterative in nature, because as your business solution develops, some unidentified risks become more obvious.

Stage 2: Carry out qualitative risk analysis

The objective of this process is to prioritize the identified risks to the probability of their likely impact on your proposed business solutions objectives. This process has the capability to rate risks into high risks that may require top priority response strategies, medium risks that will need to be kept on the watch list and low risks that need to be monitored.

Stage 3: Carry out Quantitative Risk Analysis

The purpose of carrying out quantitative risk analysis is to further analyse the risks more objectively so that you will be able to rate them numerically on how they could affect your overall business solutions objectives. Although, quantifying the risk dose not reduce the potential damage the risks are likely to cause, but one important benefit of this process is that it helps reduce uncertainty in your work. One important way of carrying out the quantitative risk analysis is to do sensitivity analysis and representing your results on a **Tornado chart**.

The sensitivity analysis is an iterative process that involves investigating how changes in one of the variable will affect an outcome when all the other variables are kept constant and then repeatedly changing another variable while keeping all the others constant. This is done in order to determine which of them will have the greatest impact on your business solutions objectives.

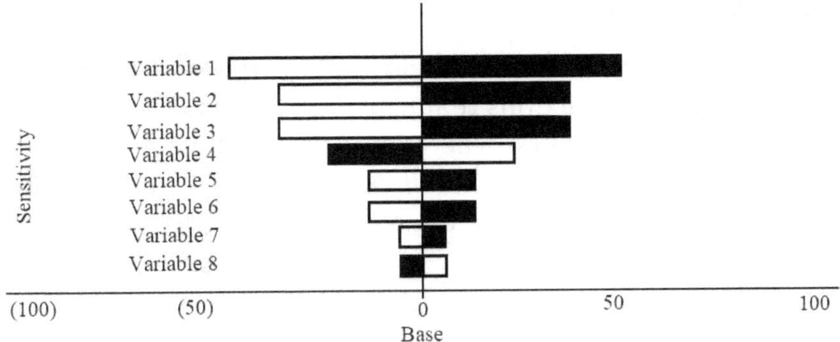

Figure 13. Tornado Chart

As seen in the figure above, the results represented in a tornado shaped diagram provides several useful information. Firstly, it helps you identify which risks are most important so you can focus more effort on and developing strategies for managing them. It also identifies whether the positive impacts out weights the negative ones.

For example, if your business requires quick delivery systems and you do a sensitivity analysis on reducing costs by the means of transportation. In your test, you decide to cut costs by making use of cars/ship to send your items over long distance rather than to use planes, you save costs by using shipping of cars but risk having late delivery dates that may seriously affect you relationship with your clients and therefore you tend to lose customers at the expense of saving money on transport.

<u>Plan risk responses</u>

As the name implies, it is the process of developing adequate options and possible actions that can and will be taken in an event an identified risk occurs. The main aim of this process is to enhance the opportunities identified in the SWOT analysis with the aim to reduce the treats to the business.

For example,

If there are positive risks/ opportunities, you plan your response towards:

- Exploiting the risks/ opportunities

- Accepting the risks/ opportunities

- Sharing the risks/ opportunities

- Enhancing the risks/ opportunities

However, if there are negative risks/ threats, you plan your response towards:

- Avoiding the negative risks/ threats

- Transferring the negative risks/ threats

- Mitigating the negative risks/ threats

- Accepting the negative risks/ threats

Make a summary budget for the business

In this section, you will need to factor in the costs attached to developing your business solution, product or service. Here, each activity will be analysed and all necessary resources required to complete the activity will be put into consideration and then you develop a draft of your summary budget for the proposed business solution, product or service.

Make a list of relevant stakeholders

The stakeholders we are referring to in this section are those persons or group of persons who may have a positive or negative impact on the success of the development (or sales) of your business, product or service. They may also be those that may be affected positively or negatively by your business, product or service. They include:

- Those group of individuals who are actively involved in developing the business.

- Those group of individuals whose interest will be affected by the work being carried out.

- Those group of individuals that exert a level of influence on the development of the business or the completed business.

- Those potential customers that will patronise the business, buy/use the product or service etc.

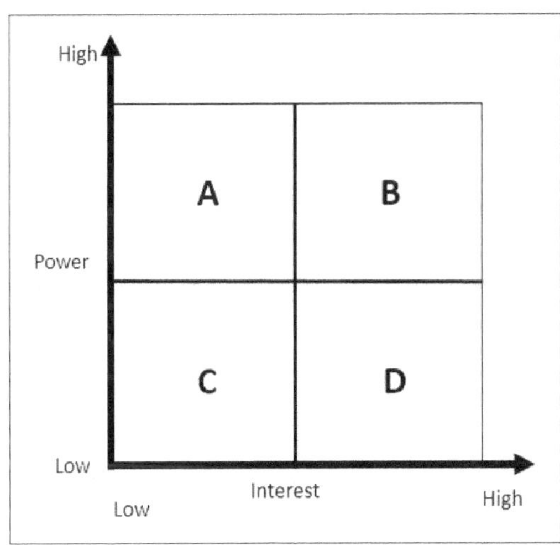

You then use the power/ interest grid to analyse and classify these stakeholders. By doing this, your main aim is to:

- Identify and classify stakeholders with respect to their relevant information such as their interest, expectations and influence etc.

- Which one has most interest, expectations and influence on your business?

- Which stakeholders interest, expectations and influence etc. is top priority to satisfy

This will enable you properly prioritise things more connected to the stakeholders who are most important in respect to interest, expectations, power etc. This is done such that you can put all necessary things in your business, product or services in place, integrate all the necessary parts and sections in your business, product or services such that you meet their expectations of those stakeholders most important to you.

Make a brief summary of activities, schedules and milestone

This draft is important as it contains one of the most important parts that will ultimately serve as a guide used in setting up the business, product or service in the later part of this book. It should contain the following:

- **List out each activity**: list of activities that are required to create the business, product or services

- Sequencing the activities: here, we are concerned about logically arranging and sequencing each task such that the accomplishment of one task will kick off the start of the next task

- **Resources**, Time scale and milestones: here, you are meant to identify all necessary resources that is required to successfully complete the business, product or services these include things like equipment, supplies or materials, estimate these resources (in terms of quantity) required to perform each task/activity, carry out a brief analysis of how long each activity will take setting out milestones are required points

- **Costing**: here, each activity is taken into consideration and its associated cost to complete the activity is analysed and documented.

Phase	Activity	Resources	Date
Phase 1, Starting point	Kick off	*Man power & time, money & equipment*	*January 1, 2017*
	Collect general data for product development	*Man power & time, money & equipment*	*February 1, 2017*
	Develop Product Scope	*Man power & time, money & equipment*	*March 1, 2017*
	Develop accompanying Product documents	*Man power & time, money & equipment*	*April 1, 2017*
	Complete accompanying Product documents	*Man power & time, money & equipment*	*May 1, 2017*
Phase 2, Product planning	Conduct Market Research	*Man power & time, money & equipment*	*June 1, 2017*
	Develop Market Research Report	*Man power & time, money & equipment*	*July 1, 2017*
	Make essential drafts	*Man power & time, money & equipment*	*August 1, 2017*
	Develop Product plan	*Man power & time, money & equipment*	*September 1, 2017*
Phase 3, Product development	Carry out activities to develop the product	*Man power & time, money & equipment*	*October 1, 2017*
Phase 4, Product Monitoring	Monitoring the product development to ensure its compliance with the initial plan	*Man power & time, money & equipment*	*November 1, 2017*
Phase 5, Product Review	Review all activities and make corrections where necessary	*Man power & time, money & equipment*	*December 1, 2017*
Phase 6, Complete work	Complete product	*Man power & time, money & equipment*	*January 1, 2018*
Phase 7, Launch	Launch the product to the public	*Man power & time, money & equipment*	*March 1, 2018*

Write out what constitutes success criteria

In developing this section of your work, you have to spell out specifically what constitutes a success criteria for the whole business and if possible, do this for the end of each stage of the development. If your success criteria is clearly spelt out, it helps you build consensus in members of your development team and also keeps your experience on track. Ensure all write-up is documented for reference purpose.

By developing this write-up, you will have to give each stage a set of success criteria that should have the following characteristics:

- The success criteria should be clear

- The success criteria should be Simple not complex

- The success criteria should be straight forward

Some examples of success criteria include;

- My product or service should offer a better customer experience than my competitors

- My products should have faster booting time

- Fewer steps to access my service compared to other clients including home delivery service.

- Customers should be able to easily get my products conveniently without stress etc.

Other Important drafts

Other aspects to be developed include:

- Draft of the business assumptions and constraints

- Location for the business

- Number of staff to employ

- Opportunities where the business can take advantage of or benefit from new technologies

After this has been put in place, the next stage is to develop the business plan.

Sections of the Business plan

As earlier mentioned in this book, the business plan is meant to provide a vision and clarify the strategy that will be used in the business. In other to do this, it should be properly developed with the following basic outlines.

1. Executive summary

2. Company description

3. Products/services

4. Market analysis

5. Strategy and implementation

6. Organization

7. Financial plan and projections

Executive summary

The executive summary is the part of the write up that is meant to introduce you and your business to the proposed audience (e.g. an investor). The main aim of this section is to draw the reader to your company so that they will want to read more about your company. It appears first in the document, but ideally it should be written last in the development of the plan. This is to ensure that you pick brief information of practically all aspects of the business plan.

Ideally, the executive summary should also include:

- The name of your business

- The location of your business

- The products and/or services offered by your business

- The company's mission statement

- The purpose of your plan which may include

- o How you intend to secure investors

- o Business set strategies

Company description

This section of the business plan should provide a high level overview of your company. It is meant to briefly inform the reader who you are and what you do in the business, how you plan to operate, what are your goals, when the company was formed, etc.

Ideally, other sections of the Company summary will also include:

- A brief history of the business

- The type and legal form of your business e.g. sole proprietorship, partnership, etc.

- The nature of the business and the needs the business intends to satisfy/address

- A brief overview of the products/services, customers and suppliers of the business.

- A brief summary of the company's growth, financial and market highlights.

- A summary of the short-term and long-term goals of the business.

Products/services

This section of the business plan should describe what you intend to sell in the business. It is meant to provide the reader with a list of products and services you sell and if possible, provide a brief description of them. The idea here is to focus your attention on customer benefits.

Tips to help you develop an attractive business plan include:

- Adding pictures and diagrams to throw more light on your explanation

- A brief explanation on the market role of your product, goods or services

- Advantages it has over other products in its competition

- If possible, information on the life cycle of the product

- How much the product, goods or services will cost and how you plan to deliver it to potential customers

Market analysis

In this section, you need to have a good knowledge and understanding of your industry. Based on your market research, you need to provide a brief description of the industry, its dynamic nature, where your customers are, how you plan to reach out to them and deliver the product, goods or services.

Ideally, other sections of the market analysis will also include:

- An illustration depicting size, demographics, groups, potential and targeted customer segments

- Statistics and outlook of the industry

- Past, present and projected marketing information for your product/services

- A detailed evaluation highlighting possible strengths and weaknesses of your competitors in the industry

Strategy and implementation

This section of the business plan should describe the strategy you intend to use for the business. It should describe the innovations that will make your business outstanding, the approach you will use to attract your target market, and how you intend to keep and maintain a loyal customer base. Tools to help you succeed in this aspect includes schedules with dates, budget, and various planning tools.

Ideally, sections of the Strategy and implementation will also include:

- Details about pricing of products, goods or services, promotions and distribution

- Brief overview of how the company will function throughout all the operations, i.e. from procurement of supplies all through to manufacture and product delivery

- Important information on sources/types of labour and the required number of employees needed for the business

- Important information on working hours and facilities with which the business will operate

Organization

This section of the business plan should illustrate and provide a brief description of the organisation of your business, the key members of your management, your organisation structure, and their functions, board of directors and their background and experience.

Ideally, sections of the organisation will also include:

- The organizational chart of the business containing descriptions of the various departments and important employees

- A list of the business advisors, board members, accountants and legal representative.

Financial plan and projections

This section of the business plan should provide a description of projected cash flow tables, profit and loss and all assumptions made during the projections. This section should be developed by a professional accountant or with their support and technical expertise. It should contain balance sheets, sales forecast data and a break-even analysis.

Other parts also include:

- Prospective financial information which will likely include balance sheets, cash flow statements, forecasted income statements, and capital expenditure budgets for the next couple of years

- A brief analysis of your financial data, featuring a ratio and trend analysis for all financial statements

Developing your Marketing plan

This is supposed to a different phase of the business, however, due to cost implications, it will be best suited to include this in the planning stage of the business. A marketing plan can be described as a blueprint of how you are going to put your marketing strategy and tactics into practice. It is very important that every business has a marketing plan. If your business does not already have one, you can use this book to serve you as a guide to developing a simple marketing plan for your business today.

A good marketing plan should be clear and set SMART objectives that will help you achieve both long term and short term goals. It is meant to give you good directions on things like:

- Your strengths compared to your competitors

- An idea of who your best customers/clients are

- What seems to be working for you and how you can get more of your best customers/clients?

- How you can keep your existing best customers/clients happy

- In order to communicate my business in a dependable and convincing way, I need to put together certain systems and standards in place. What are they?

- What are the best types of marketing styles will most effectively reach my target market?

- Do I need partnerships to ensure success in the marketing? If so, with whom?

It does not have to be a long complex document. At first it is important you develop the plan keeping it simple. Once the plan is developed, you can then systematically modify it adding more information to it as you acquire more information from your marketing environment.

Things you need to do before you develop a marketing plan

One important thing about the marketing plan is that it ensures that all the team members are aware of what they are required to do and how they are going to go about it to make it successful. However, if this is going to be effectively accomplished, it is important that one embarks on the following studies:

- A study should be carried out to **Review the existing marketing environment of your business.** This study should include a thorough analysis (internal and external) so that you can gain thorough knowledge of your strengths and weakness in other to gain more knowledge of your market environment and identify more market opportunities for your business. An example of the tool that may be used here is the SWOT analysis tool that can be seen in the previous sections of this book. Examples of your strengths may be good location of sales outlet, products and services have very good pricing compared to your competitors, etc.

- A study should be carried out to review your business, product or service from the customer viewpoint (Thinking outside the box). This information needs to be gathered using various techniques like surveys, focus groups, interviews, brainstorming sessions etc. The questions are intended to pick the customers brain to provide answers to questions like:

  o What is the customer really looking for in your business, product or services?

  o What benefits does your business, product or service offer to the customer. Is it what the customer really want?

- A study should be carried out to review the target markets. Your target customers may be local or international. They may be local if you operate a retail location sited within the neighbourhood or international if you sell to customers internationally online. This study should include a thorough analysis so that you can gain knowledge of any additional products or service your business can offer to the target markets or any other additional market your business can tap into.

For example, you might want to find out if there are any similarities between the targets customers e.g. are you customer women because you only sell women cloths. If so are you going to tailor more of your services to the female gender or do you want to venture towards men apparel... etc. you can develop a tool that may be used to help you in this activity is the use of the excel sheet seen in sections.

- A study should be carried out to review the existing marketing environment of your business. This study should include a thorough analysis (internal and external) so that you can gain thorough knowledge of your strengths and weakness in other to gain more knowledge of your market environment and identify more market opportunities for your business.

- A study should be carried out to investigate the strengths and weaknesses of your existing and potential competitors to your business, product or services. This study should be reviewed from time to time (e.g. annually) as it will continually equip you with the necessary knowledge so that you can improve your position in the market/industry.

- A study should be carried out to review the existing marketing environment: by his, you will have to study your current situation and developing trends, economic, cultural environments, etc.

- A study should be carried out to review the existing marketing mix the 7P's: These includes things like the

  - Price

  - Product i.e. the business, product or service

  - Promotion i.e. advertisement and other ways you can get your business, product or service known to the public

  - Placement outlet where the product will be sold

  - People

  - Place

  - Process i.e. the extra value added services that are being offered by your product that gives you an edge over your competitors' e.g. home delivery or after sales services.

  - Packaging i.e., the quality of the packaging

- It should also be worthy of note to

  - Look closely at your competitors and what they are doing and how they are carrying out their marketing plan

  - Study their networking styles, where and when they network

  - Make a list of outlets where you think you can market your goods and services

  - At what price do you think that you can tag your products that will be to your advantage?

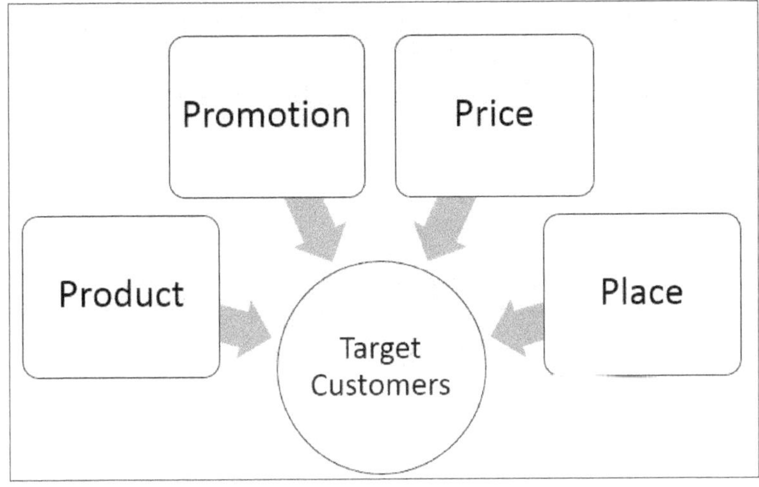

Here your study should make emphasis of appropriate linkages between the decisions you make, the marketing plan, each P in the marketing mix and your target customers.

Contents of your Marketing plan

Now that you have done the preliminary studies, the next thing to do is to put together your contents of the marketing plan. Here, the plan should be properly written and it has to be clearly spell out what needs to be done and the outcome of each task or activity should be easily quantified such that the performance can be monitored.

Marketing plans may come in simple or complex, small or large number of headings. For example, a small business may have description, marketing budget, and description of the business location, pricing strategy and possibly the market segmentation as outlines. A more complex marketing plan for a large scale organisation will go into more details of the above mentioned and also have additional outlines like financial forecast, Controls, etc. Basically, it is usually best to start it simple and if the need be as you progress in development stages of the work, you use progressive elaboration to add more fields and information to the existing ones to build it up. The basic contents of a marketing plan should contain but not limited to the following sections:

1. The Title page

2. The Executive Summary

3. The current situational Analysis

4. Current and potential opportunities

5. Aims and objectives

6. Marketing Strategy

7. Action Program

8. Financial Forecast

9. Controls

Developing your Sales Plan

This section may also be simple or complex document, however, here idea is to keep it simple. The questions your sales plan should be answering should include but not limited to the following:

- How you intend to promote your product or services?

- Who are your target market?

- Where are your target market located?

- What are the existing and potential channels of distribution you intend to use?

After the planning and development stages of the work, you should have developed the following:

- Business plan

- Marketing plan

- Sales plan

Furthermore, by now, you are expected to have a vivid idea of what you intend to do and how you are supposed to go about it. Also, at this stage, all this information you would have gathered should be adequate for you to design a prototype or service for testing. The next thing to do is to search for partners and suppliers.

Chapter Five: Strategic approach to finding partners and suppliers

Partnerships

A business partnership may be described as two or more persons coming together to establish a business with the sole aim of making profits. It may be seen between professional services engineers, doctors, lawyers and accountants etc. Here, these partners share their expertise, skills and workload organising work schedules for the success of the business.

How partnerships are made

There are different ways a partnership may be formed. It may be formed by a handshake, it may be formed orally or it may be formed via written partnership agreement. The written partnership agreement is usually developed by lawyers. However, if a partnership is not formed via written partnership agreement, it may easily lead to misunderstanding and disputes.

Find partners and suppliers

In this section, we are considering the different types of partners and suppliers including the individuals or group of people with whom we intend to work with in order to sell our products or services.

Here, we explain what you are to search for in a partner or supplier, where you are expected to find them, how to plan the relationship, conflict and manage communications.

Having a good product does not guarantee that you will be making very good sales. One very important aspect a lot of business owners fail to take into consideration is finding reliable and efficient partner who will deal with the wholesale aspect of the business at the right price.

Once you have gotten assurance that this aspect has been straightened out, you can then start considering issues related to quality and standard control, terms of trade and available options for delivery.

Factors to consider when seeking partners and suppliers

In selecting a partner, it is important to take into consideration some important things like:

- Price, speed and reliability
- Experience
- Checking the company history
- Alignment with your business
- The Risk factor

Price, speed and reliability

In selecting a partner, it is important to consider a balance between Price, speed and reliability. Some partners may offer a low price but may not be reliable or even meet up with the speed in the demand for your goods and or services. Others may offer reliability and speed but may charge too much for the job. It is important that you make a balance in these three angles of the triangle sorted in order to get a good partner.

Experience

Organisations with a good number of years of experience have a reputation to protect, as such they operate with high quality standards whilst offering reliable services. They also have experience in dealing with unforeseen mishaps that may prop up along the way.

In selecting a partner for your business, it is important to select one with a good number of years of experience in the industry as this will increase your chances of success in your endeavour.

Checking the Company history

In selecting a partner, it is worthy of note to check the past history of the organisation. This is because, you would not want to mortgage the future of your great product or service with a scam company or an organisation with a very bad history in dealing with clients and customers.

Alignment with your business

In selecting a partner, it is worthy of note to check among the list of your potential partners to find out which one aligns more closely with your business, product or service. This will go a long way to aiding the success of your business. The following should be carefully considered:

- Are the potential partners aligned in the same industry?

- From their previous activities do you see them as inclined to your kind of business?

- Do you have similar interests or are they interested in helping you grow your product? If so how can you both benefit.

- Are they interested in learning more about your customers?

- Have they been involved in any form of promotion to help your type of customers or business?

The above questions will go a long way in helping you land the right partner for your business.

The Risk factor

In selecting a partner, it is worthy of note to check with the potential partner whether your partnership has the potential to mitigate any significant risks for the partner.

Here, you need to identify how your business will fit into the partners operations without additional costs or bottlenecks to their operations.

This is an important aspect of strategic alliance as it may help both parties bring about significant cost savings and accelerated product development.

Common Problems associated with partnership

Though partnership helps build businesses, if it is not done right, it negatively affects the business which in line may affect the quality of service and may end up ruining the entire business venture. Some of the problems likely to affect a business partnership may include:

- One partner may feel he is doing all the work and the other is just ripping all the benefits.

- Expectations of both parties in the partnership are not being met due to poorly structured partnership arrangements.

- A partner may lose interest in the business venture or decides to change to another type of business.

- Poor communication between partners

- Completely wrong selection of partner.

How to find partners and suppliers

The most common and simplest way to find a partner or supplier is to use the simplest traditional method "Asking" other business owners how you can get partners and suppliers. It's not rocket science and when you have the funds and all the big business ideas running wild in your mind, people may tend to forget some simple and common things available to them. Other ways of finding partners for your business include:

- **Government directories**: in most countries of the world today, there are special government directories that contain list of businesses, organisations, suppliers, manufacturers and other different types of companies. When searching for partners and suppliers for your business, it will be worthwhile to get a copy of this directory and search for partners or suppliers.

- **Trade associations**: getting access to Chambers of Commerce, Industry, Mines and Agriculture of the particular country where you are located is a very good way of getting access to partners and suppliers. Identify with them, arrange for a meeting and you will be surprised at the much help you can get from them.

- **Newspapers and magazines**: Getting a copy of business magazines that are related to your niche is one way of getting partners and suppliers. A lot of these partners and suppliers usually advertise on these magazines. Get hold of the magazines and call them.

- **Trade fairs and exhibitions**: Events of this nature are usually packed with partners and suppliers. Visit one and interact with them.

If you are already in business and have a partner, then it is time you carry out a review of that partner to investigate their performance. If their performance is satisfactory, one should know that business is dynamic and will not remain the same in the next 5-10 years as such find out ways you can improve your performance. If their performance is not satisfactory, then it's time you start hunting for a new partner.

Chapter Six: Strategic approach to getting funds

Even though that there are many kinds of financing options in the world today that require business plans, the honest truth is that business plans do not generate business financing. Why most investors in the world today require a business plan as a document that will pass across the ideas and information to the potential investor, the real deal is that the investor invests in a company, product or individual.

Research has shown that in order to succeed at the early stages of your business, you need to put aside just enough funds to start the business and comfortably operate it for at least three months. Some other researchers peg this time frame for at least six months. This funding should comfortably cover start-up costs, running, operating and expenses for the stipulated time period.

Challenges to getting funding for your business

This matter is rather touchy as it appears to be somewhat complicated rather than stressful in its terms. Getting finance to start your business is not a stroll in the park as investors will be sceptical about releasing funds for you. Some of the reasons include:

- Lack of experience

- Poorly developed business Plan

- No assets

- Wrong figures in your estimations

Lack of experience

Studies have shown that, in trying to convince an investor to invest in your business, one key question they ask themselves in their mind is whether or not you have the experience to do what you actually say you want to do or whether investing in you will be a profitable venture or a waste of resources.

If you are a man, they may be wondering whether you are old enough to deal with such responsibility, and I if you are a woman, they may be wondering if you are strong enough to deal with challenges when they arise.

In a nutshell, investors want assurances, and by this we mean that you show confidence, have realistic plans, projections in both cost, risk, revenues and profits.

Poorly developed business Plan

When you are trying to get funds off an investor, it will be worthy of note to remember that you are being evaluated on how you make your presentation and also on the way you present your business plan. If you are not confident in your presentation and your business plan is not properly put together, or if he feels the slightest sign of doubt in your package, he will not risk investing in your business.

No assets

Assets serve as a form of security for the investor in an event that the funds collected cannot be returned. In some instances, if you do not have any assets, it may be difficult getting an investor to buy into your business.

Wrong figures in your estimations

Some investors may go the extra mile to check the figures you present to them in your plan. If they decide to go through your documents and they find that the figures you have given them is incorrect, they will not invest in your business, thus, it is important to recheck the values and figures you put in the data you hand in to the investors.

Channels to getting funding for your business

These are several channels one can get funding for your business. Below are a list of a few channels one can get funding ether for a new or existing business. They include:

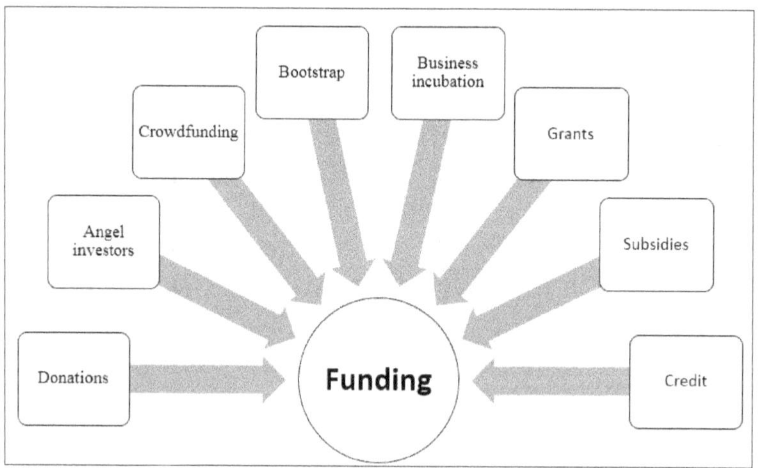

Angel investors

This can be said to be investors that provide finance for small businesses at the start-up phase. They may come from family members, friends, colleagues etc. In some cases, they are believed to be investing in the individual rather than in the business. They are also believed to be inclined to be helping the business succeed and expecting small percentage in return for their investment usually between 20 – 30%.

Crowdfunding

This can be said to be the type of fund raising whereby the funds needs to setup the business venture is raised by a large number of people. It is usually done over the internet and it is usually comprises of 3 different stakeholders;

1. The initiator of the business who has the idea

2. The people or group who arc in support of the idea

3. The organisation who bring together the initiator of the business and the group who support the idea and create the platform to launch the business idea

Bootstrap

This can be said to be a situation whereby the individual who has the business idea decides to start the business with his own personal finance. Here, he explores every available options to him in order to raise the money needed for the business. The initial capital is usually not very much and the business owner maintains control over all decisions in his business. The challenge with this system is that the capital may not provide enough investment for the business to hit a very successful start and this may place some avoidable financial risk on the business owner.

Business incubation

Business incubator can be said to be a company that helps new businesses or small start-ups grow by providing these businesses with some essential services and support through the initial vulnerable stages of the business. The support they provide may be in form of provision of office space, reliable internet facility, training, customer service help desk, etc.

Other forms of raising capital for businesses include: Factoring, bank overdrafts, cash advances, asset-based lending, peer-to-peer loans, micro-loans, community scheme, family loans, government grants, barter, winning a contest, etc.

Once we are done with this part of the work, the next thing that needs to be in done is to set up the business.

Chapter Seven: Strategic approach to Setting up the business

Seeking counsel

This is about the final stage involved in getting the business up and running. At this point, the business owner should seek counsel from his advisors. This includes his legal, accountant and other advisors in his list. The reason for this is:

- To seek counsel from your adviser/consultant as this will help you address all the dose and don'ts and the rules and regulations you need and all the necessary paper work to protect your business.

- To seek counsel from your adviser/consultant to help you address all the grey areas in setting up the business.

- This advice will also help the business owner to work out which legal structure is right for him, register for tax etc.

After seeking counsel and advice, the business owner should review all the plans and be sure you are comfortable with the list of activities, their sequencing, time scale, milestones, costing and all other plans you have initially put together to ensure they are realistic and practicable to him.

Factors associated with business failure at this stage

- Improper planning

- Lack of stakeholder involvement

- Unclear objectives

Setting up the Business

There is a popular adage in my country that states, No be only one road dem dey take go market"... Meaning: "there are different routes one can use to get to the market". You can get to the market from the North, South, East, West, South - East, South - West, North - East, South - West etc. Either way, all we are interested in is getting to the market. The same applies to setting up the business. There are different approaches you can use in setting up your business. You may decide that you want to use a simple approach, or you may decide you want to use a very complex approach. The choice is yours. However, it is important to develop a document that will guide you through the actual work that is required to put that idea into the market, this document is called the business project management plan (BPMP).

Development of the BPMP.

In this book, we will integrate some practical approaches and the strategic approach provided in developing a business (which can also be called a project) as mentioned in the PMBOK guide. The document will be called the business project management Plan (BPMP).

The BPMP is the document that will describe step by step all the stages involved in the entire project lifecycle which invariably consist of all the work that is required from the conception of the idea, to bringing the product to the market. If it a service we are providing, we are considering all the document that will describe step by step all the stages involved in the work that is required to make the service into operation.

Contents of the BPMP

All the information earlier gathered in the previous sections of this book will be reviewed and its entirety, developed in sections to form a guide and documented in the form of the BPMP report as seen below.

- BPMP

- Scope

- Milestone list

- Schedule

- WBS

- Procurement

- Cost

- Quality

- Risk

- Resource

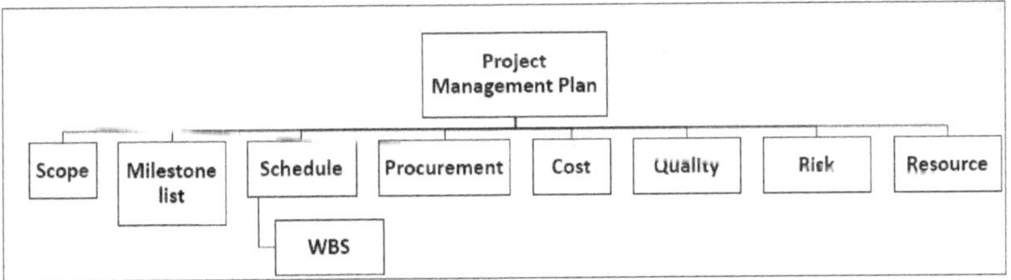

It is this document that describes how the work will be executed, monitored and controlled in other to complete the deliverable.

Another important aspect of this document is that it provides a document that the project team can fall back to for reference reasons so they can consult in case the work is going out of scope, budget, quality and time.

While the scope sets the boundaries where you should not exceed or go beyond, the scope management plan provides a plan to help you work within the scope boundaries and also serves as a guide to help you return back to the scope in an event you wonder off the scope of the work.

The Milestone list will provide a list identifying all milestones in the development of the work.

The Schedule presents linked activities information of the entire development with planned dates, durations, milestones etc.

WBS (Work Breakdown Structure) provides information on the breakdown of all the work required to be carried out to develop the deliverable.

Procurement and Procurement management plan provides procurement and Procurement management related information for the successful completion of the work. It also provides information of how you will acquire products, services, equipment's and others for the successful completion of the deliverable.

Cost and Cost management plan provides information on how the costs will be planned, structured and controlled for the successful completion of the deliverable.

Quality and Quality management plan provides information on how the quality will be planned, structured and controlled for the successful completion of the deliverable.

Risk and risk management plan provides information on how risks that may positively or negatively affect the successful completion of the deliverable will be planned, managed and controlled.

Resource: this has information on how the resources will be planned, managed and controlled.

Strategic approaches to setting up he Business

<u>Strategic approach I</u>

This approach is pretty much straight forward. It requires that the business owner constitutes a development team and uses the approach of starting the work by putting together plans to organise and prepare for development. The team then commences the execution of all the work and related tasks required to develop the work. The team then ensures proper monitoring and control of all aspects of the work to ensure compliance to the stated deliverable. After completion, the team then closes the work and opens the business up to the public.

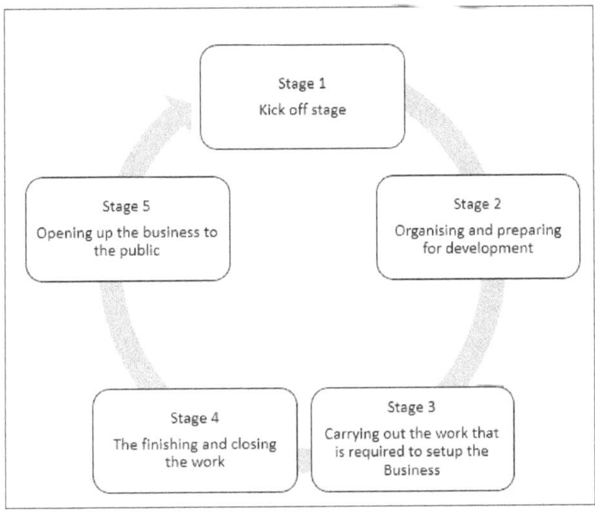

Here, the stages include:

- Stage 1: Kick off stage

- Stage 2: Organising and preparing for development

- Stage 3: Carrying out the work that is required to setup the Business

- Stage 4: The finishing and closing the work

- Stage 5: Opening up the business to the public

The success of the work will be measured in terms of achieving the said aims and objectives as stated in the business solution and in terms of completing the work on time, budge and quality within the constraints of the scope as earlier defined.

Strategic approach II

This approach is a bit more complex. It requires that the business owner also constitutes a development team whose sole duty is to complete the deliverable and get it into the market.

This strategic approach uses the Scrum model to setup the business. Here, we view three (3) stages which include, the pre-game, the game and the post-game stages.

- The pre-game phase

- The game phase

- Post-game phase

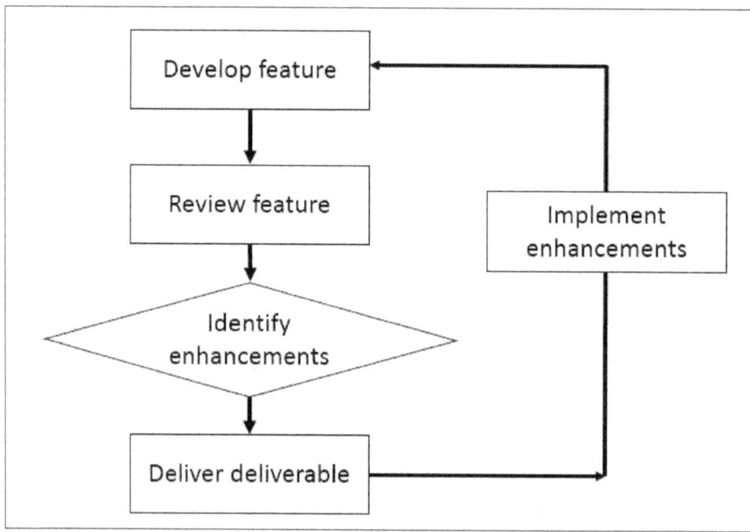

The pre-game phase

This is the first stage of setting up the business. It requires that the business owner, after thoroughly perusing all the business documents previously prepared in the previous sections of this book, kicks off the predefined plans and actions required to will finally put the business into the market.

This stage is done by the business owner with help of an industry expert and possibly a potential customer. They collaboratively work together to identify the most important requirements/features that the business, product or service should have. These features are then prioritises according to their level of importance to the business and then documented as the goals and put together as the business backlog document (BBD). During later development of the business, this BBD will continually be updated as more refined information becomes available during the development of the business. During this stage, it is important that you keep your focus not to get out of the focus of your scope.

The business owner in most instances will need the support of a group of individuals to help him setup the business. These group make up the development team and will ensure completion of the work. It is important that this team is made up of industry experts and one or more professionals to aid in the development of the work. They will then be designated the developers. It is a combination of the development team that will be required to determine what and what is needed and what functionalities they will be needing to develop the business, product or service. It is also their job to determine release dates, reiterate the scope of work, quality and budget required and if any additional support required for the success of the business.

The game phase

This is the second stage of setting up the business. This is the iterative process involving the actual development of the business. It requires that the business owner follows plans and actions specified in the pre-game phase to develop the business. It is realised in what the scrum process describes as sprints. Each sprint is meant to produce a reasonably releasable business or product. If the business, product or service meets the business owners specifications, then the business owner may decide that the end of the business development has reached and he can go ahead to launch the business, product or service. However, if he feels that this is not the case and he feels that the business, product or service has not yet reached the stage where it should be released, the business solution is reviewed, additional features added and updates made to the BBD then another sprint is ensured.

During this stage, they are three activities that takes place. They include Formulates a sprint goal, Develops the sprint backlog and Estimates tasks.

Formulating sprint goals

During the formulation of the sprint goals, the development team develops a comprehensive description of resources it requires, activities that needs to be carried out and what it needs to be done and what needs in order to successfully carry out a sprint. All these are the formulation of a sprint goal. In essence, in establishing sprint goals, it requires that the development team states the outcome by describing what is required to complete each sprint.

Developing the sprint backlog

During the development of the sprint backlog, the development team determines what and what needs to be done in order to develop the backlog item. It then puts them together and develops a list to be used during each sprint. This list comprises of a list of tasks and activities required to develop the backlog items.

Estimates activities and tasks

As the development team finished determining the backlog items, it then categorizes these items and breaks them into smaller tasks and groups for more effective work. It then makes an estimate of what efforts need to achieve success.

Where there is need to make a change in the features in the business, this is carefully considered by the owner and the development team before this in implemented. In most cases, it is advised not to change the features that have been earlier stated in the initial business plan. This is because it may affect the scope, however, it is only advisable to involve changes when it involves instances where high-priority change or omission has been identified.

Now, during this time, there are some important points to consider:

Timing: The time required to setup the business as earlier mentioned in the previous sections of this book has to be refined based on deliberations on the actual work to be done and conclusions from meetings by the development team in the development of your business solution. This has to be agreed upon and followed judiciously so that the work will be completed having the approved quality, on time and budget. The job may last between 1 – 6 months or even more depending on what was specified in the meetings.

The actual deliverables: What is to be developed may be to setup the business, develop a product or service. Whatever the endeavor is, it will be termed the deliverable and it is during this stage that all the work as earlier specified must take place to successfully complete all the deliverable. The success criteria should be used to measure success of the work after completing to ensure that the deliverable should be fully developed and tested against all backlog items, and meets the business owners requirements and at the right quality.

Meetings: whether it is a regular meeting or a review meeting, it is important that the development team have meetings at regular intervals. At these meetings, there information is exchanged, options evaluated and decisions are arrived at. These meetings are used to address and discuss important issues that relate to the progress and completion of the work. If and when there are issues to be dealt with, it is via these meetings that the matters trashed out. Whenever there problems, it is via these meetings that the problems are reviewed and solutions developed.

After each sprint, a review meeting is ensured to find out if the deliverable meets the specified completion criteria. If the deliverable does not meet the completion criteria, there is a review of the product backlog, and another sprint is ensured. This process is repeated iteratively until the business owner is satisfied that the deliverable has met the specified completion criteria. If so the work ends there and the business or product is prepared for lunch.

The post-game phase

In the Scrum approach, any work needed after a sprint or after a series of sprints is called the post-game phase. Since the aim of each sprint is meant to provide a complete deliverable, the business owner ought to be satisfied with his newly completed deliverable as such, if the sprint is implemented properly, there is no post-game stage.

If the business owner is not satisfied with the completed work, he identifies errors, lapses or possible improvements and then tasks his development team to carry out another sprint iteratively until he is satisfied with the deliverable.

Some companies also use this strategic approach to gain customer loyalty and better still add a little innovation to make a lot of profits by releasing a series of multiple products. An example can be seen in the mobile phone industry whereby a model is released the previous year, the development team then works on the lapses, adds a little innovation, make improvements and then release another product the following year. They repeat this over and over, year after year and by the time you realise it, they have provided quality products, put together a respectable brand and provided high level of customer satisfaction raking in billions of dollars.

<u>Strategic approach III</u>

This approach is also a bit complex. Here the business owner constitutes a development team whose sole duty is to complete the deliverable and get it into the market.

The approach here is that the development team builds the business and then starts operation. During this stage, testing is simultaneously being carried out to understand the customer reaction to the new business. It is the customer response that is then gathered and taken back to the drawing board. While the business is still running, improvements are then made based on information collected from the customer and then further improvements are made on the business and then released. This process is repeated iteratively until the business owner is sure that he has gotten exactly what he feels the customer wants.

Features of this approach includes;

1. Building

2. Start

3. Test

4. Making adjustments and revisit your plan

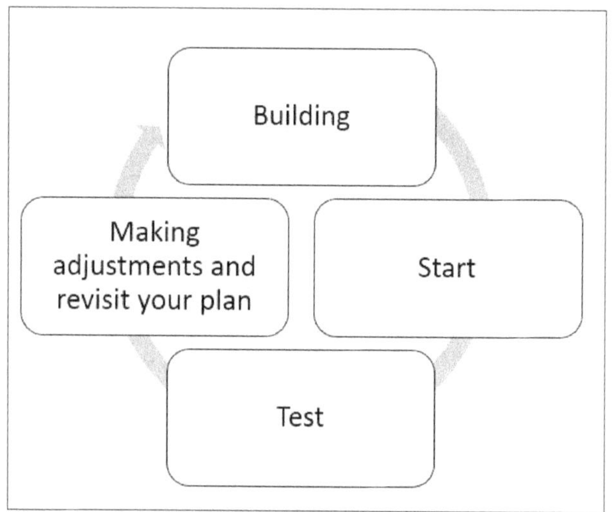

Building: This refers to the main product, goods or service you originally intend to offer in your business. It may have several features in which you originally have in mind however, it is very important to focus mainly on features tailored to address the needs of your customers in the simplest form. This can then be developed accordingly with the most economical means as possible.

Start: This refers to opening up the outlet and exposing your goods and services to the market. It is a common say that perfect is a formidable enemy of good enough, as such you must not wait until your product, good or service is perfect before you take it to

130

the market. You need to take it to the market the moment you and your advisers feel the product, good or service is good enough for customers. The moment this is done, you ensure you keep an eye open for feedback as this will serve as a means of learning how you customers are reacting so that you can modify the product, goods and services appropriately.

Test: This refers to testing elements lake features, customer experience and pricing so that you have the advantage of matching your product, goods or services with customer experience. Once this is ensured, you then identify and seek ways to repeat successes records and cost effective strategies used that produced favourable results for you and document findings.

Making adjustments and revisit your plan: This refers to repeating more of the things you did right that produced favourable results and tweaking / using newer approaches to the things you feel you did wrong that wasn't favourable to your business. You then revisit your business plan and update appropriately. You can then proceed to growing the business by seeking new investors to increase financial support to grow the business.

Activities that take place in this section

As earlier mentioned, setting up a business is a project as such should be treated as one. The activities that take place during this stage includes:

- Doing the actual work that is required to produce the deliverable (i.e. business, product or service)

- Monitoring the work, ensuring that adequate controls are put in place for the success of getting your deliverable.

For example, you want to start an online shop for the supply and sales of computer hardware, software and accessories. The deliverable is the website, while the tasks required to setup the website include designing the website, developing the codes, putting together the content for the website, putting together your price list etc.

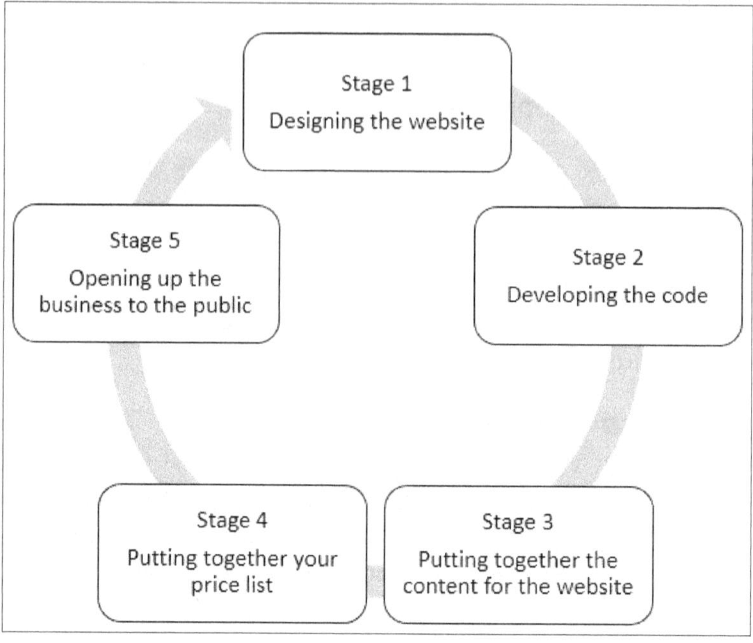

As seen in the example above, these tasks as earlier specified would have to have been written out, listed out, sequenced, time scale and milestone made out in your planning stages of your work.

Now it is time for you to proceed and do the actual work that is required to be done in other to produce the deliverable. The activities are as follows:

Perform all the tasks as stipulated in your plan:

- **Perform all the work packages**: This entails that you perform all the work packages as described in the BPMP regarding all the business activity list in accordance to timelines to create the respective deliverables (Business, product or service)

- **Meetings**: Conduct regular meetings with your team mates to ensure that you communicate the progress of the work as described in your plan to ensure that the work is going on as described in the business plan and timelines

- **Reviews**: Conduct regular reviews with your team mates as stipulated in the business plan and timelines

- **Audits and Inspections**: Carrying out audits, inspections and analysis as stipulated in the plan to ensure things are going on as planed

Ensure adequate Monitoring and control of development

- Monitor all the tasks as stipulated in your plan and ensuring proper controls are followed as stipulated in the plan

- Ensure that the business, product, services or result matches what the documented scope.

- Ensure that the actual schedule, timelines and milestones are properly monitored and compared with what was written in the plan to ensure that things are going on as planed and on target.

Chapter Eight: Strategic approach to Growing the business

Now that you have succeeded in starting up your business, you start making sales. The next important thing to start doing is growing this new business. Just like in using the computer, you are told, garbage in equals to garbage out, Input equals to output. This is somewhat similar to your business. You are bound to get the resulting output of what you put into your business.

A lot of people might like your business, product or service, but for a client or customer to walk into your organisation and carry out one transaction like purchasing a product and leaving the organisation may not necessarily sustain your business.

In other to grow your business, there are certain things that need to be thoroughly considered. They include:

- You should lower your barriers of defence and understand that you must have to be open and willing to receive feedback.

- Seek advice from your mentor.

- You have to do away with your pride (not entirely but to a greater extent).

- You should ask questions that will invariably open your mind to a better understanding to what you are into.

- You should have trust and confidence and trust in yourself.

- You should be ready to explore all available opportunities to help your business or organisation grow and be ready to sacrifice and willing to make important changes.

By doing this, you are creating the perfect environment for tremendous growth beyond your wildest imagination in your business or organisation.

Furthermore, there is the need to explore some strategic approaches in growing your business. These include approaches like:

- Finding ways to integrate your business into the supply chains of other businesses

- Going into discussions or partnering with other businesses that offer similar products (but not necessarily the same thing) and making them offers with your products

- Seeking creative ways of getting clients and customers to patronise you (like offering bonuses and customer rewards)

- Design and development of innovative advertising systems etc. the list goes on and on...

It is a known fact that business owners are constantly trying to make profits in their endeavours as this is beneficial to the survival of the business. They get so caught up with the activities of buying and selling that they have little time to settle down to think on how to grow their businesses. This is a challenge not usually faced by larger companies as they usually have a budget set aside to acquire the services of a consultant who will advise them on strategies to growing their businesses. Let us take a look of some reasons why people may want to grow their business.

Reasons why you may need to grow the business

Business growth may come naturally. A booming business at one time or the other usually get to a point where growth is inevitable. One of the major reasons for growing a business is for more profits. However, there are several other reasons why one might consider growing the venture. They include:

- Better edge to compete favourably amongst its competitors

- More and more profits

- Better and more professional staff

Better edge to compete favourably amongst its competitors

The idea of growing a business generates more attention for the business and creates more opportunities for improved profits for the business. Growing a business gives the business an edge to competing favourably with other competitors in its market. It also raises the chances of the business qualifying as a primary supplier for larger Corporations.

More and more profits

Growth in business usually records increase in profits. This profits can be used at a later date when there is an unexpected loss in the business. The previous profits recorded can then be used to cushion the effect of the loss to make more profits.

Better and more professional staff

A growing business will attract more professional staff. This gives the business owner more choices to select from several professionals. Having professionals handling your business gives you a certain level of relief compared to armatures.

Factors affecting business growth

Business owners who only recently setup businesses wish their businesses will grow. However, businesses being a very complex endeavour has a lot of challenges. There are several factors known to influence the growth of business ventures. They include:

- Available funding for business growth

- The presence of new competitors in the market

- Advances in technology

- The introduction of new products

- Available Staffing and other essential resources

Insurance for the Growing Business

Growing a business often comes with some associated risks, as such, care should be taken to cushion some effects by putting in place plans to address risks that may be associated to liability loss, income loss, property loss or even people loss.

Strategies used in growing businesses

While strategies used in growing businesses have changed over the years, companies have continued to focus on high levels of employee relations and customer service.

Over the years, different approaches have been used to analyse various strategies that organisation use to grow, however, one popular strategy used by many organisations is the Igor Ansoff's matrix (Igor Ansoff's 1965).

<table>
<tr><td colspan="3" align="center">Increasing risk →</td><td rowspan="4">Increasing risk</td></tr>
<tr><td>Product

Market</td><td>Existing products</td><td>New products</td></tr>
<tr><td>Existing markets</td><td>Market penetration</td><td>Product development</td></tr>
<tr><td>New markets</td><td>Market development</td><td>Diversification</td></tr>
</table>

As seen in the figure above, this matrix considers the levels of risk and opportunities associated with new products within new markets. Based on this information, four strategies may be observed. They include:

1. Market penetration

2. Market development

3. Product development

4. Diversification

Market penetration

This strategic approach is based on the introduction and sale of more products into the existing markets. In most cases, the price of the product or services is reduced or the company increases investments embarking on more promotions in other to gain more customer awareness and increase sales.

Product development

This strategic approach is based on the development of new products and services. These products and services are then introduced into the market.

Market development

In this strategic approach, the organisation takes an inventory of all its products and services, studies a new market and make a selection of its products and services that may likely sell in the new market and introduces them into the new market.

Diversification

Diversification can be described as a high risk corporate strategic approach used by companies to venture into a new market that it was previously not into before. It may do this by creating a new product or service. In most cases, the company does not have any experience in this new market and does not have any idea if this new product or service will be successful at the end of the day or not.

Some examples of the strategic approaches used in growing the business include:

- Opening another location/branch for the business

- Offering the business as a franchise for other investors

- Partnership with other businesses to form alliance

- Introduction of the sale of complementary products or services

- Introducing importation and exportation in the business

- Strategically targeting other markets

- Merging with or acquiring other businesses

- Expanding the business globally by the use of internet and other available means

- Rebranding

As seen in the above strategic approaches, it is important to note that a careful study of customer demands in the market usually brings about the need to introduce new products or services. Based on this fact, it is evident that the widening of the organisations scope across new markets and other sectors may start in form of product or brand extensions with the main purpose of adding new products into the market. These strategic approaces have recorded increased patronage over recent years and can be seen in some major organisations today.

Strategic approaches used in entering into foreign markets

The world is considered a global village by many, as such, many Companies and organisations all over the world are increasingly entering into the foreign market as it is important for the growth and the survival of the company. This is also known as internationalization. In most cases, they engage in this practice to increase their profits, market share and capital to stay ahead in their competition in the industry. Some of the strategic approaches they use to achieve this includes:

- Franchising

- Exporting

- Licencing

- Greenfields investments

- Strategic alliance

- Give away dealerships

Steps required to growing your business

Based on information provided in the previous sections of this book, it can be seen that there are bits and pieces of information that can be combined in thousands of different ways in other to achieve your objective in this section (Growing the business). However, it can be seen that there will be need for proper documentation if the work will be successfully completed. Find below some steps that have been extracted from this book that have been discussed in more details in the previous sections of this book.

Steps required to growing your business

Stage 1

- Identify all the stakeholders

- Carry out a marketing research and document your findings. Carry out some investigations to Identify possible activities that will need to be done to grow the business e.g. questionnaire, interviews, brainstorming, consulting experts in the industry, focus groups, etc.

- Develop a Business development plan

    o Business analysis

    o Business goals Setting

    o Business objectives setting

- From the information gathered during this stage, you carefully develop a draft of what you propose to do

Stage2

- Develop a plan of what you want to do. This plan should constitute the following:

    o Identification and making a list of all tasks and activities that are required to do in other to grow the business

    o Logical Sequencing of all tasks and activities required for the success of the work

    o Making a list of all the resources required for carrying out the task

    o Estimating time required for carrying out each activity and coming up with a schedule and milestones

    o Estimating costs associated with completing each activity.

Stage3

- Start doing what you have set out in your plan

    o Perform the tasks required to make the deliverable

    o Ensure adequate Monitoring and control of the development

Stage4

- Review, and if required redo some of the tasks

- Carry our quality assurance

Stage5

- Complete the work and sign off

Hands on

Based on the information provided in this book, a number of volunteers were brought together from a bakery that had previously recorded low patronage. They carried out a brief research based on the steps provided in this section in the growth of their business. The information below provided a brief summary of some of the activities (some information was withheld for reasons not given to us) that ensured.

Stage1

- They carried out Stakeholder identification which includes the following:
  - Their neighbours
  - Government regulatory bodies in their locality
  - Environmental Health and safety inspectors
  - Their competitors
  - The general public (Potential customers)
- They then carried out a marketing research and document your findings. Here they carried out some investigations to identify possible activities that will need to be done to grow the business by the use of questionnaire, interviews, brainstorming sessions and by consulting experts in the bakery industry.
- They then developed a Business development plan
  - Conducting a brief business analysis
  - Setting business goals

○ Setting business objectives

They then developed a draft of what you propose to do from the information gathered. These were what they proposed to do to grow the business:

Stage2

- They developed a plan of what you want to do. This plan was made up of the following.

  ○ Identification and making a list of all tasks and activities that are required to do in other to grow the business. Among the list of activities, some include the list on the table below.

S/No	Activity/task	Duration
1	Improved interaction with customers as this will help create a connection between the customers and the operators of the bakery for getting easy feedback.	6 months to 1 year
2	Advertise the bakery products on various ways like local TV stations, Newspapers, radio, print media etc.	3 months
3	Promote the bakery products on various social media platforms like Facebook, Instagram, twitter etc.	Continuous/ongoing
4	Increase the number of customised bakery products on our shelves. By this we mean identify the products which our loyal customers patronise and try to innovate more products like it and increase the numbers of such products on your shelves	Continuous/ongoing
5	Open your doors so that the smell of your products will diffuse out to the neighbourhood	Continuous/ongoing
6	Establish new training sessions in the establishment. This will include baking classes for some of our top selling products	Continuous/ongoing
7	Make offerings for bakery products that have stayed overnight e.g. you can give a 40, 50 or even 60% discount for products that have not being bought the previous day. Then if they are not sold, remove them from the shelf. You can also setup a local neighbourhood food bank charity where by you give away a day old bread	Continuous/ongoing
8	Identifying and meeting with restaurants, caters and hotels around their locality and offering wholesale of backed products.	Continuous/ongoing
9	Provision of new baking services (collaborating) for events like weddings, birthday parties and other social events	Continuous/ongoing

- o They then logical sequenced all tasks and activities required for the success of the work

- o They then made a list of all the resources required for carrying out the task

- o They then estimated the time required for carrying out each activity and coming up with a schedule and milestones

- o They then estimated costs associated with completing each activity.

Stage3

- They then started doing what they had set out to do in their plan

  - o They performed all the tasks required to make the deliverable making adjustments where necessary

  - o They ensured that there was adequate Monitoring and control of the development

Stage4

- They reviewed, and re-executed some tasks

- They carried out quality assurance to ensure quality was given top priority on the output of the work

Stage5

- Complete the work and sign off

For a bakery located in a good part of town that previously had little customer base, the resultant effect of this work recorded a huge increase in their customer base and in profits.

Hands on

Some examples of themes where these strategies have been successfully implemented in the past.

S/No	Industry/Focus area	Activity/task	Solutions
1.	Security	Lack of funds to • Address staff salary • Operations cost • Government Tax's	• Prioritizing tasks and activities and using the funds to address top priority matters • Reinvesting funds back into the business
2.	Security	Personnel • Getting the right people to do the job • Effective management of these people • Getting people who share your vison	• Start small, get key people and train them to share your vision • Partner with people in terms of service • Practice the reward system so that staff are being rewarded based on performance

Chapter Nine: Strategic approach to Business optimisation

Against the backdrop of the continuing climb in Unemployment and poverty faced by many countries in the world, starting up a new business, growing it and optimising existing businesses is becoming an ever more attractive proposition to support governments in creating employment and in aiding economic growth and development of the country.

If properly explored, the idea of optimising a business can help larger organisations support the local economy by developing the rural regions and also strengthen small and medium-sized businesses.

Optimization can be defined as the act, process or methodology of making something more effective with better results or making it as good as possible. Business optimisation can be said to be the act of making the business more productive and as successful as possible. The approaches here refers to the strategies in which one will use to achieve the above goals and objectives. One prevalent strategy used by most professionals in this field is known as Kaizen.

Before we dive into Kaizen proper, we will first take a look at some focus areas organisations have placed emphasis in implementing Kaizen for continuous improvement that has brought tremendous success. They include focus areas like:

- Placing more emphasis on outcomes and results

- Integrity

- Passion

- Appreciating your staff

- Benchmarking and optimisation

- Make working in your business fun

- Staff Training

- Employing the right people and creating a balanced team

Placing more emphasis on outcomes and results

It is a known fact that people spend their money to purchase positive outcomes and results. These includes things like solutions or answers to their problems, value, advantages, improvements, time saving, avoidance of pain, protection, benefits, pleasure, fulfilment, enjoyment, prestige and things of these categories. By changing strategy to focus on the improving, promoting and selling these outcomes and results to the customers, one notices that there is increased customer satisfaction and profitability.

Integrity

Just as integrity is defined as the quality of being fair, honest or complete, it is important that when dealing with customers and employees likewise, we should constantly improve on our integrity in our businesses. This approach to our business practice takes the customers interest ahead of your own, and further produces the attitude that creates an enabling environment for your business to thrive with great success.

Passion

It is a known fact that people tend to be attracted to someone passionate about the activity he or she is engaged in. There are several ways one can explore passion for the benefit of improving your business. These includes:

- Showing passion and being passionate about your business. This on its own is a motivation for you and your business in its entirety

- Motivating your employee to work with passion strategically attracts more clients that see this genuine burning desire in you and your employee which in turn is systematically optimises performance in your business.

- Being passionate about your customer's needs and use of your product or service. This may be achieved by starting up passionate discussions with your customers on better ways to use your product or service, hidden features to improve its usability and possible improvements the customers wish the product or service can possibly offer.

Appreciating your staff

This is one very important strategy used by some of the most successful companies in the world today. In most cases, it comes in form of a kind of compensation for hard work by the company to that individual or bonus pay on the dividends of the annual sales to staff at the end of the year. When you genuinely appreciate your staff, they tend to be more dedicated, happy and satisfied with their work. Benefits attached to this include:

- Your staff tend to turn up to the office on time

- You have a high rate of staff retention mean that you enjoy the benefit of keeping a more experienced workforce.

- More customer satisfaction

Benchmarking and optimisation

Benchmarking can be said to be for one company to study successful business practices of fellow competitors and implementing some of the ones you consider may be applicable and will work in your own company or business, these include things like successful business practices that others competitors have already confirmed, successful systems of operation etc. By this, you are saving your company a considerable learning curve.

Similarly, with respect to optimisation, you make a careful study and selection of all successful systems that have previously applied with confirmed successes with maximum returns on least investments in time, capital and human resources in your organisation. You then integrate them to your current systems and apply and reapply for optimal results e.g. prioritising tasks and activities such that you use funds and other resources to address top priority tasks/activities first before dealing with others.

Make working in your business fun

Make working in your business fun refers to the instance where get your staff involved in building an enabling environment to encourage play, fun and laughter at work. Here, it is important to carefully implement strategies to build an enthusiastic high performance team that will integrate good morals in your business or organisation. This creates a good corporate culture and ultimately increases productivity in your business.

Staff Training

The importance of staff training in optimising businesses performance cannot be over emphasized as it affects everything about the business and makes an enormous positive difference on how everything works in the business. The benefits include:

- As you train your staff to perform much more advanced tasks, they become better and produce better results which ultimately gives your business an edge over your competitors giving you better optimised performance bringing more profits to your organisation

- It helps your staff better understand the objectives of the business better and improves the standards in your business, IMPROVES problem solving and ability to address customer complaints more effectively lending to improved profits.

Employing the right people and creating a balanced team

Employing the right people is employing people with the right qualification and experience. Also, this refers to placing square pegs in square holes and placing round pegs in round holes. By this we mean you employ according to profession as this gives you better chances of specialization and success. Employ and place a marketer in a marketing department and an Engineer in an engineering department.

Kaizen

This section is designed to provide support, fill up existing gaps in knowledge and provide strategic approaches to aid employers and employees through the various planning phases of the optimisation process through to realisation of their goals (Business optimisation).

Kaizen on its own is a very large area of study and will not be covered in debt in this book. There are several books in the market that covers this subject in depth. However, this book introduces you into the subject and enlightens you on how to optimise your business for improved efficiency, effectiveness and eliminate activities that do not necessarily provide value to the process. It will also provide you with strategic approaches to taking sound actions to reduce defects and improve customer satisfaction.

Definition: Kaizen is a Japanese word broken down as Kai meaning change, Zen meaning good. Kaizen can be said to be the practice of continuous improvement. Continuous improvement can be said to be the ongoing improvement of a business or its process, product or services. It is used in a lot of companies and conglomerates as an important part of their long term competitive strategy. The process was made popular in the Toyota production system where all personnel were made to stop their current production system when a problem was observed. They were then meant to suggest improvement via the kaizen cycle and then resolve the issue or implement an improvement as seen in the figure below.

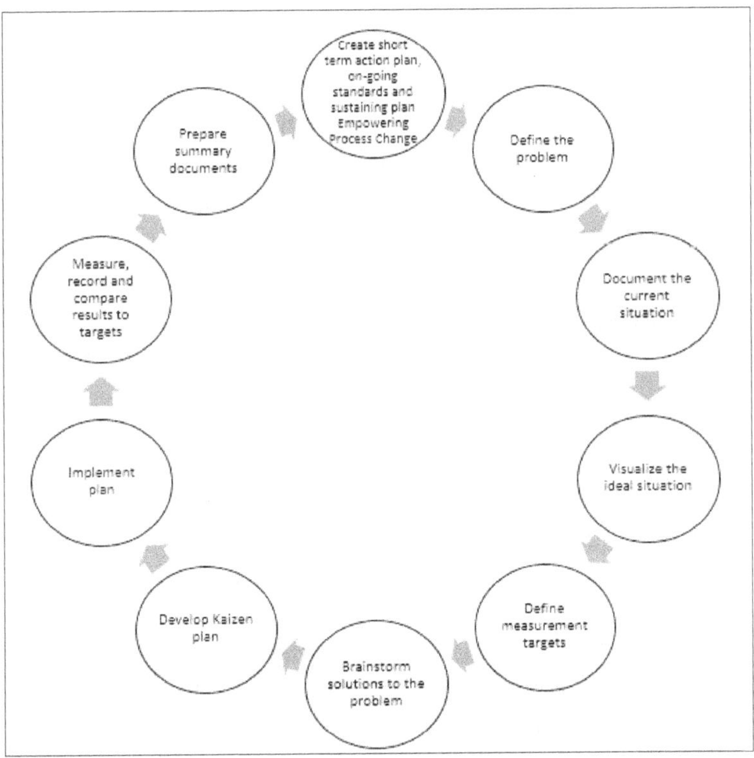

The stages include:

1. Create short term action plan, on-going standards and sustaining plan empowering Process Change

2. Define the problem

3. Document the current situation

4. Visualize the ideal situation

5. Define measurement targets

6. Brainstorm solutions to the problem

7. Develop Kaizen plan

8. Implement plan

9. Measure, record and compare results to targets

10. Prepare summary documents

The method relies on group effort comprising of small steps done many times in an iterative style. If it is done correctly, Kaizen humanizes the workplace by teaching people using scientific methods on how they can carry out experiments on their work to eliminate hard work, learn on the spot and improve business processes by way of elimination of waste, improvement in quality and productivity and the efficient use of resources.

Principles of kaizen

- Improvement using Kaizen brings to us an understanding that good processes will bring about good results

- Improvement using Kaizen brings to our knowledge that improvements in an organisation not solely comes from deliberations being made from the conference room, but rather, improvements is every body's business

- Improvement using Kaizen helps us to understand that it is important that we make immediate corrections to mistakes and errors as soon as they are found

- In order to improve your business, you have to keep asking why until are aware of the problem, then you take action to contain and correct these root causes of problems

- Improvement using Kaizen encourages that you all have to work as a team

- Improvement using Kaizen helps you understand that for effective improvement, there is no room for blame

- In Kaizen, you must not wait for complete perfection in the improvement, rather if you can achieve 50% development, you are making progress

- In Kaizen, Everyone involved in the work is supposed to be made to understand that there should all think positively rather than thinking negatively e.g. By saying we cannot do it

The Kaizen approach

The strategic approach of Kaizen is that everyone in the business or organisation is to be made to understand that it is their individual responsibility to identify inefficiencies in every area of their work and suggest positive improvements where ever necessary to move the organisation forward.

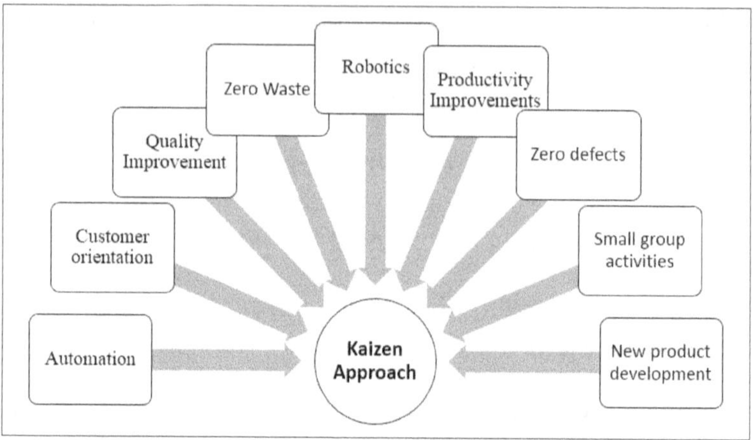

As seen in the figure above, some uses strategic approaches which highlights improvement areas such as, automation, customer orientation, quality improvement, zero waste, robotics, productivity improvements, zero defects, small group activities, new product development etc.

The approach of Kaizen typically aims for improvements that all eventually translate to savings in terms of finance and consequentially converting potential losses to profits for the business or organisation. The approach are not limited to, but include:

- Ensuring that resources and employee skills are used more efficiently as possible in other to reduce waste from all activities and processes

- Ensuring that staff motivation is given top priority such that they are satisfied and are kept engaged as this is a drive for them to remain with the business or organisation.

- Ensuring that customer satisfaction is also given top priority by the provision of high quality products that have fewer or no faults

- Training and retraining of staff on problem solving skills so that each individual member of staff contributes to the growth of the organisation by providing solutions to problems in their respective areas of specialization.

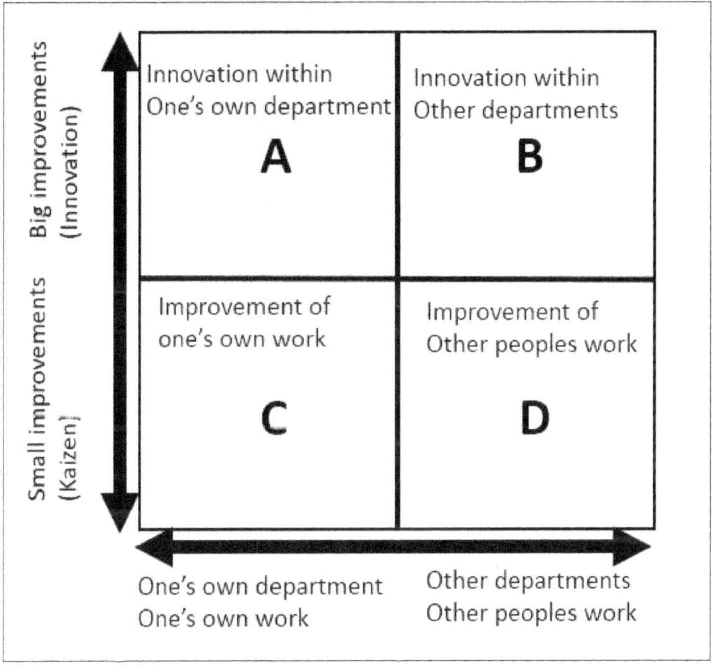

- Encouraging team work and ensuring that the management makes effort to develop strong teams that to address more complex problems in the organisation

- Increasing efficiency by encouraging competition such that higher quality products are produced at lower costs

- Ensuring that staff have more stake in what they do such that they become more committed to their tasks and inclined to improve on their work to provide better results

Some key issues that require clarification before Kaizen implementation

If an organisation is planning to implement Kaizen, there are some key areas that require sound and adequate clarification. Even though these areas may already be understood by the group, it is still important to reiterate their importance to them for smooth sailing of the work. These key areas include:

- Developing a business optimisation work breakdown structure (WBS)and reiterating its importance

- Reiterating clear roles and responsibilities

- Timeline, schedules and milestones (The when)

Developing a business optimisation work breakdown structure (WBS) and reiterating its importance

Extracts from the PMBOK Guide reveal that the WBS visually breaks down the whole work to be carried out in a hierarchical manner and organises it into smaller manageable jobs that can be easily understood by the team for easy access and understanding.

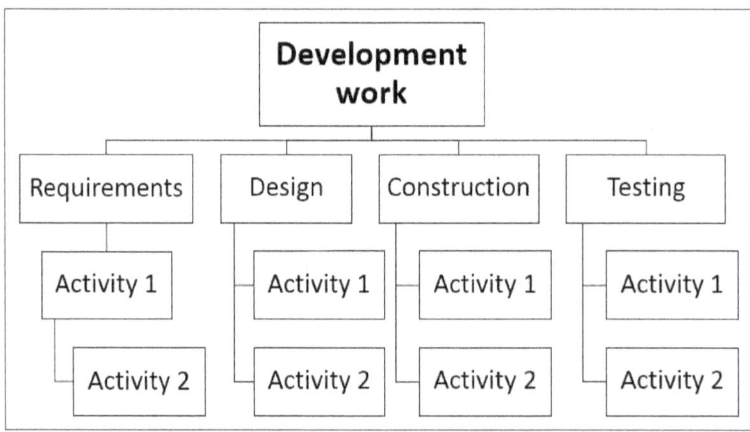

If an organisation is planning to optimise its business, product or service using the kaizen strategic approach, it is important that the organisation uses a sound integration of focus areas, kaizen principles and approaches to develop a simple AP. It is this simple AP that will then be further developed into a more detailed AP and then afterwards, a WBS will be developed and used to further break down the whole work to be carried out in a hierarchical manner that will organise the activities and tasks into smaller manageable jobs that can be easily understood by the team for easy access, understanding, planning and implementation.

Reiterating clear roles and responsibilities

Depending on the size of your business or organisation you are looking to optimise, it will obviously have different needs of the type of individual's roles and responsibilities. If it is small, it may not require a complex structure, however, if it is large, it may require a complex structure in the roles and responsibilities.

If an organisation is planning to optimise its business, product or service using the kaizen strategic approach, it is important that the senior management responsible put together a Project Optimisation Team (POT) making clear the roles and responsibility of each team member. This may include; assigning a team leader, team members, subject matter experts, facilitator, process owner etc. furthermore, it is important to develop and document their role descriptions and clearly stating their roles and responsibilities. See brief explanations below:

The client/Customers

This can be described as the people why the business optimization process is done because of them. They are those group of people whom are directly going to use or benefit from the goods, product or services after the optimisation process.

The designer/developer

In the process of planning to optimise your business, there are different potential solutions that are likely to meet your customer needs, however, the designer is the person who takes time to study the optimisation strategies and selects the best optimal approach to be used in achieving the objectives. On the other hand, the developer is responsible for building the solution designed by the designer.

The Suppliers / Vendors

In the process of planning to optimise your business, it may sometimes be necessary to get input from suppliers and vendors. These are basically suppliers and vendors that supply hardware or software that will be used in optimising the business process. There may be some new innovations, upgrades or even advanced systems at a lower cost that may greatly aid you in achieving your goal.

The Subject Matter Expert

This refers to the expert that has the knowledge of a particular field area of specialization or discipline in a particular part of the optimisation process or in all aspects of it.

Timeline, schedules and milestones (The when)

A milestone can be said to be a significant event or stage in the progress or development. In this business optimisation assignment, in the duration of each activity, we attach start and finish dates, resource as well as budgetary allocations to all activities and deliverables that are meant to be completed in the business optimisation project.

Strategic approach to Kaizen Application

The first thing to do is to set up a project optimisation team (**POT**). The purpose use the team is to use the Plan Do Check Act (PDCA) system of approach to optimise the business.

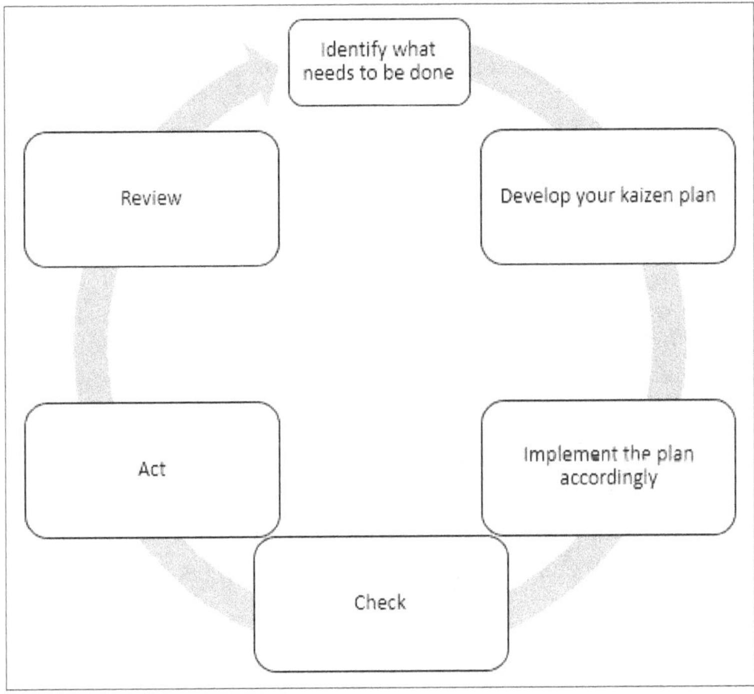

As seen in the figure above, the optimization will be:

1. Identify what needs to be done

2. Develop your kaizen plan

3. Implement the plan accordingly

4. Check

5. Act

6. Review

Identify what needs to be done

The first task of the POT is to identify all what needs to be done and document it. This is likely to include a brief or narrative description of the possible outcomes or results to be delivered by the tasks. The POT then designates tasks or carry out the process.

With respect to the selection of the individuals responsible for this work, it is very important that the person or group responsible of making this decision carefully select individuals who are the most qualified and talented who possess the essential skills, those that are most motivated, most passionate about this work.

The POT then visualizes what needs to be done, establish the scope of the work and set boundaries and limitations that will not be exceeded in the work to be done. The POT are responsible for making assumptions at this stage and be clear about them. It should be noted that this process will be fashioned out to be iterative in nature as further adjustments and updates will be made as you progress in the optimisation process.

The questions and possible answer may start with:

✓ What you want to do? You want to optimise the business.

✓ What and what results do you hope to achieve: here it is advised that you develop a list. These may include things like

- o Better customer satisfaction

  - ▪ Produce better quality products

  - ▪ Produce products with less defects, fewer or no faults

- o Benchmarking

  - ▪ Research and implement successful systems and verifiable practices used by my competitors

  - ▪ Research and start giving out special offers used by my competitors

- o What are the resources you think you will like to be used more efficiently as possible and reduce waste

  - ▪ Finances

  - ▪ Man power

  - ▪ Time

- o What are the employee skills you think you will like to be used more efficiently as possible?

  - ▪ Problem solving

- o What are the waste you would like to reduce from all activities and processes?

  - ▪ Finance

- o What ways do you think you would like to motivate your staff better?

  - ▪ Salary and rewards

  - ▪ Training and retraining of staff

- o What teams do you think is necessary to develop and improve in your organisation?

    - Adhoc teams

    - Market and marketing research

    - Business development

  - o What ways do you want to use to ensuring that staff have more stake in what they do such that they become more committed to their tasks and inclined to improve on their work to provide better results

    - Encouraging staff involvement and participation in developing improvements in the business

- ✓ Who are the people involved

  - o Customers

  - o Staff (From top management executives to the assembly line workers)

  - o Supply chain including partners, suppliers and others external to the organisation

- ✓ Where is this optimisation to take place?

  - o My business premises/organisation

- ✓ When

  - o Set a time frame with which you will like to achieve this optimisation e.g. 2 years.

- ✓ Why

  - o Complete business optimisation of business, process, quality etc.

The POT then carry out a marketing research and document your findings. Carry out some investigations to Identify possible activities that will need to be done to grow the business e.g. questionnaire, interviews, brainstorming, consulting experts in the industry, focus groups, etc.

- Develop a Business development plan

    o   Business analysis

    o   Business goals setting

    o   Business objectives setting

- From the information gathered during this stage, you carefully develop a draft of what you propose to do

Planning

The POT identifies all aspects of this optimisation process (most likely as listed above), decides the approach to be used by the POT in achieving the above objectives and develop plans of how the objectives, deliverables will be met. In this case, we are also concerned with the why, what, who and when.

- The "why" being the first part of the job i.e. business optimisation process

- The "what" being to identify what needs to be done and the POT develops planning data for the actualization of the goal

- The "who" is all the roles and responsibilities i.e. people that will be involved in the business optimisation process.

- The "when" meaning that we have to attach timelines and milestones to certain work to be done

- Spell out their roles and responsibilities

- Develop a business optimisation work breakdown structure

- Develop timeline, schedules and milestones

Do

In this section of the work, the POT implements all the plan by executing the process exactly as it was written in the planning stages in other to complete all work. The tasks here include:

- Doing all the work according to the schedule listed in the plans

- Ensure that you purchase all the necessary items, equipment and supplies that will be required to optimise the business process

- Doing the right thing to ensure that top quality guidelines are followed

- Conducting Inspections, as well as reviews and validations in a timely manner as it has been specified in the plans to ensure all aspects of the job is carried out in the right quality standards are followed and met

- Carrying out regular audit of the work to ensure things are going on as planned, making all the necessary adjustments and ensuring high quality standards are met

- Ensure that all team members make use of all specified quality measures as specified in the business optimisation quality control measures

- Again the implementation of Kaizen to ensure you reduce waste and eliminate all other unnecessary processes that do not add value to the process

The POT members

- Reiterating that tasks that needs to be accomplished by all team members, re enlightening the on all activities and milestones, and ensuring all members of the team understand what needs to be done and keeping them focused and informed on their development

- Having continuous and regular meeting to ensure that every one is kept up to date on new developments

    o Carrying out regular and continuous updating of team members of important milestones that have been achieved

- Ensure that as the work goes on, you continuously improve knowledge, cohesion and dynamism of all team members

- Ensure that as the work goes on, you manage the team members to ensure there are not conflicting issues, and if per adventure it pops up, quickly address these issues.

- Overall, there should be proper information generated in this "do" process and ensure that the right information is communicated amongst each and every team members

    o These may include formal or informal communication channels, communicating delivery status, and cost of development so far, schedule and milestone progress made thus far.

CHECK

The word here is measuring performance. The key objectives of the check stage is basically to recognise any deviation in the actual work execution process from the planned one and perform corrective actions to realign the work for optimal performance and minimise risks.

In essence, after you collect and measure the data, it is important to distribute the data to appropriate quarters so that all possible improvements on what is done can be adequately carried out. This means that:

- You ensure that you carry out point by point review of associated deliverable

- You ensure that you that you properly measure, examine and validate areas that need to be evaluated to determine whether the work meets specification or acceptance criteria

- You ensure that you send your results for further reviews and audits to subject matter experts.

During this stage, the POT mainly monitors and control the work being carried out in the execution stage. The main tasks carried out in this stage include tracking, reviewing and reporting on the progress of the work that is being carried out to meet the objectives of the optimisation process. This means that you gather corresponding work execution data that will be used for the act stages.

There are different tools you can use during this stage to understand the deviations from the actual work being carried out. They include:

- Inspections

- Statistical sampling techniques

- Cause and effects

- Flowcharting

- Pareto diagrams

- Control chats

- Scatter diagrams

The figure below is an example of data representation from an unknown optimisation process using the control chart.

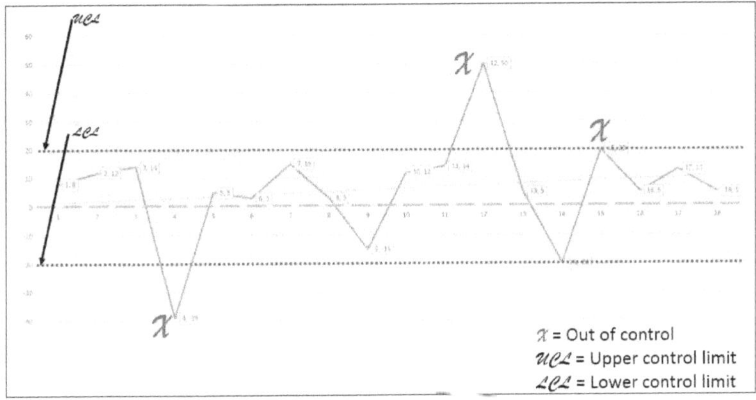

In this scenario work performance data (i.e. raw data collected from the actual executing work being performed) from an unknown process is put together and represented in a control chart as seen in the figure above. The upper and lower control limit is then set as prescribed in the BPMP. It is this information that is then compared with the initially projected results that are expected. This is done in order to ascertain the difference /variations for further adjustments to be made to meet the original objectives of the work being carried out.

In this example, it can be seen that other points fall within the control limit except for the one tagged X which appears to fall out of the control limit. In this case, the process will need to be reviewed and revisited so that proper things be put in place to ensure that all points fall within the acceptable range.

ACT

The word here is to review performance. The key objectives of the act stage is basically to learn from your mistakes and errors and from what other organisations experience. Here you revisit your initial plans and update sections of the plan where necessary. You are also meant to take actions from lessons learnt from inspections and audits carried out in the checking stage.

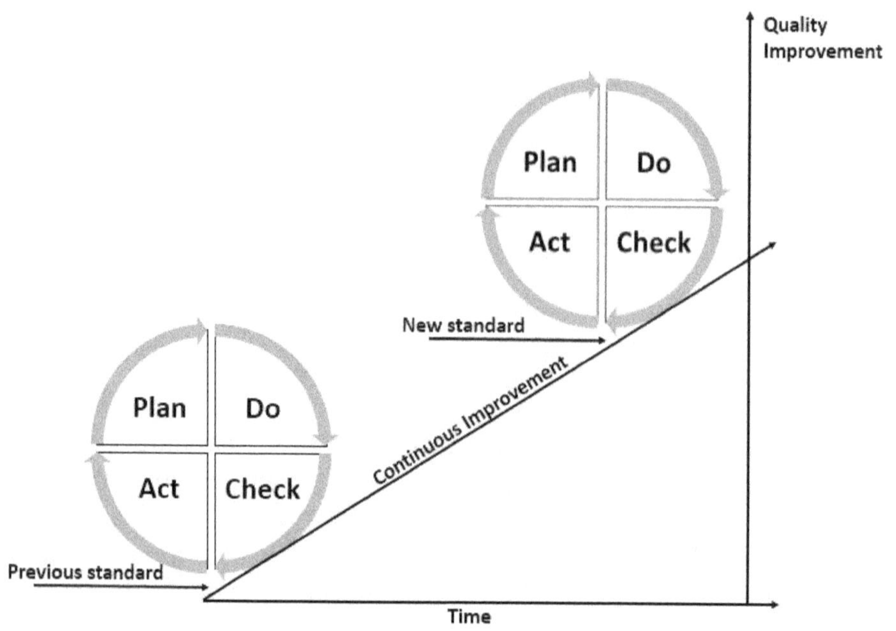

For there to be continuous improvements in the optimisations process, there are a number of areas that need to be carefully looked into. These include:

- Where new standards will have to be introduced

- No noticeable improvements

- When something new is learnt

Where new standards will have to be introduced: this scenario occurs when the check stages reveal that the plan was implemented I n the execution stages appear to be a notable improvement in the previous standards, then the POT will have to consider that this is a new standard for the team to work on in the act stage.

No noticeable improvements: If the activities in the check stages reveal that the all the plans was implemented in the execution stage and there was no noticeable improvements, that the previous standards will have to remain in place

When something new is learnt: if the activities in the check stages reveal that all the plans was implemented in the execution stage and the results appeared to be very different to what was initially expected, this may be something negative or positive, , then there is more learning to be done.

Hands on

Some examples of themes where Kaizen has been successfully applied in the past.

S/No	Industry/Focus area	Activity/task
1.	Important information boards	Rather than having a lot of information that may seem clumsy on your important information boards (meant for customers/clients, operators of machinery, visitors), you summarize, highlight and make only very important information available at a glance
2.	Call centres	Finding ways to improve all first time call resolution at your organisations call centre.
3.	Organisations	Improve communication between all levels of staff to increase awareness of organization levels, shifts and work areas.

4.	Manufacturing process	Conducting a survey of users of manufactured product to investigate possible improvements they will like to see in their products, and improving the manufactured product to meet 90% of the customer request
5.	Website sign up, update and search	Developing simpler systems that will help reduce sign up time, update time and search time by as much as 50%
6.	Staff rewards	Raise morale for staff by rewarding those that make the highest number of on-time delivery
7.	Local transport company	Rebranding the company and networking all the branches for improved communication and efficiency
8.	Sales company	Developing a comprehensive database for all customers for the purpose of effective communication and sending season's greetings and seasonal discounts to loyal customers (based on request)

In parting, I would like to remind you that it is a well-known fact that life is simple, but it is us who insist on making it complex and complicated. Furthermore, rather than dwelling on our past mistakes or worrying about the future, we should concentrate our minds and put in more effort on making a positive impact with whatever knowledge or skill we have acquired over the years and invest it in the present moment. By doing this, we will be able to make a positive impact in any community we find ourselves.

I will also like to leave you with some inspirational quotes from some famous individuals who have made a positive difference in the world we live in today.

- An organization's ability to learn, and translate that learning into action rapidly, is the ultimate competitive advantage. - Jack Welch

- Life is a dream for the wise, a game for the fool, a comedy for the rich, a tragedy for the poor. - Sholom Aleichem

- Life isn't about finding yourself. Life is about creating yourself. - George Bernard Shaw

- There are no secrets to success. It is the result of preparation, hard work, and learning from failure. - Colin Powell

- If you want to kill any idea in the world, get a committee working on it.- Charles Kettering

- There is only one boss. The customer. And he can fire everybody in the company from the chairman on down, simply by spending his money somewhere else. - Sam Walton

- Sometimes when you innovate, you make mistakes. It is best to admit them quickly, and get on with improving your other innovations. - Steve Jobs

- Strength and growth come only through continuous effort and struggle. - Napoleon Hill

- There are no great limits to growth because there are no limits of human intelligence, imagination, and wonder. - Ronald Reagan

- Intellectual growth should commence at birth and cease only at death. - Albert Einstein

- In the business world, everyone is paid in two coins: cash and experience. Take the experience first; the cash will come later. - Harold S. Geneen

References

American express. 2015. [Online]. Available from: https://www.americanexpress.com/[Accessed 16 September 2015].

Buhaug, Halvard, and Henrik Urdal 2013. An Urbanization Bomb? Population Growth and Social Disorder in Cities'. *Global Environmental Change* 23(1): 1-10.

Business dictionary. 2015. [Online]. Available from: http://www.businessdictionary.com/[Accessed 17 September 2015].

Coale, J. 1960. *Population Change and Demand, Prices and the Level of Employment.* [S.l.]: Princeton University Press.

Edmiston, D. 2007. *The Role of Small and Large Businesses in Economic Development'.* SSRN Electronic Journal n. page. Web.

Entrepreneur. 2015. [Online]. Available from: http://www.entrepreneur.com/ [Accessed 12 September 2015].

Forbes. 2015. [Online]. Available from: http://www.forbes.com/[Accessed 5 September 2015].

Inc. 2015. [Online]. Available from: http://www.inc.com/[Accessed 12 September 2015].

Napoleon Hill 2004. *Think and grow rich.*

Project Management Institute 2004. *A guide to the project management body of knowledge (PMBOK® Guide)* – Fifth edition. Newtown Square, PA: Project Management Institute.

Resource centre. 2015. [Online]. Available from: http://www.resourcecentre.gov/[Accessed 2 September 2015].

Smarta. 2015. [Online]. Available from: http://www.smarta.com/[Accessed 16 August 2015].

Start-ups. 2015. [Online]. Available from: http://startups.co.uk/[Accessed 16 July 2015].

Stephansorger. 2015. [Online]. Available from: http://www.stephansorger.com/[Accessed 4 August 2015].

The Guardian. 2015. [Online]. Available from: http://www.theguardian.com/[Accessed 11 October 2015].

Treacy, M. and Frederik D. 1995. *The Discipline of Market Leaders.* Reading, Mass. Addison-Wesley Pub. Co.

UK Govt. 2015. [Online]. Available from: https://www.gov.uk/starting-up-a-business/[Accessed 19 July 2015].

Watkinson, Matthew 2012. *The Ten Principles behind Great Customer Experiences.* Harlow: Financial Times.

World we want. 2015. [Online]. Available from: https://www.worldwewant2015.org/[Accessed 16 September 2015].

UN. 2015. [Online]. Available from: http://www.un.org/[Accessed 9 October 2015].